THE CONGRESS OF THE DISAPPEARED

Praise for this book

'The book is both product of and reaction against the "outbreak of fascism" which we experienced recently. It makes it clear that our task now is to establish enduring memory, to fight the fascism of today and organise society in such a way that fascism cannot prosper.'

Marcio Selligman-Silva, literary critic, essayist and Professor at
UNICAMP, the State University of Campinas, Brazil

'The turbulent period of the military regime should have led, amongst other things, to clear and detailed self-criticism, on both sides. But this was impossible for those who died. Bernardo Kucinski's prose drama brings back to life those men and women who never had the opportunity, in their final minutes, to unburden themselves, to settle scores, or even to make confession.'

Marcelo Rubens Paiva, novelist, playwright and screenwriter, whose own
father Rubens Paiva was disappeared under the military dictatorship.
His memoir 'Ainda estou aqui' was adapted for the 2024
Oscar-winning film 'I'm Still Here'. From 'Fantasmas
da ditadura' ('Ghosts of the dictatorship'), in Brazilian
literary review Cuatro Cinco Um

'As well as recovering historical figures and anonymous victims of the bloodthirsty rage of the repressive apparatus, the writer confidently brings out the macabre. He locates each new massacre in the parade of horrors which has been in place ever since colonial times, his use of black humour essential to describe the scale of the tragedy. It is an effective antidote to the cheap hatred of the social networks and the disgraceful treatment of these issues by the far right.'

Bia Abramo, journalist. From 'Àqueles que tombaram'
('To those who fell'), a review in Focus Brasil

'Kucinski's book, which gives voice to the disappeared, attempts to humanise them in the face of the worst barbarity. To give voice to the disappeared is one way of confronting the worst traumas of our history ... *The Congress of the Disappeared* is part of the struggle of memory against forgetting.'

'Not only does it engage with a subject of such importance, so necessary in times of neofascism, but it is such an original idea, and so well written.'

'Who better to tell the truth about their fate than the spirits of those whose bodies were never found? Their voices defy attempts to exclude them from historical records and erase them from collective memory. Their stories highlight the need to discover the truth, research what really happened, and recognise acts of both courage and cowardice, to enable those left behind to grieve.'

'The Congress of the Disappeared goes far beyond dealing with individual trauma, instead addressing the whole context of Brazil's national drama. It is Kucinski's most ambitious and well-executed work.'

The Congress of the Disappeared

A drama in prose

Bernardo Kucinski

Translated by Tom Gatehouse

LAB
LATIN AMERICA BUREAU

Practical
ACTION
PUBLISHING

Published by Practical Action Publishing Ltd
and Latin America Bureau

Practical Action Publishing Ltd
25 Albert Street, Rugby, Warwickshire, CV21 2SD, UK
www.practicalactionpublishing.com

Latin America Bureau (Research & Action) Ltd
Enfield House, Castle Street, Clun, Shropshire, SY7 8JU, UK
www.lab.org.uk

A catalogue record for this book is available from the British Library.
A catalogue record for this book has been requested from the Library of Congress.

ISBN 978-1-78853-422-2 Paperback
ISBN 978-1-78853-425-3 Electronic book

Citation: Kucinski, B., (2025) *The Congress of the Disappeared: A drama in prose*, Rugby, UK: Practical Action Publishing http://doi.org/10.3362/9781788534253

Since 1974, Practical Action Publishing has published and disseminated books and information in support of international development work throughout the world. Practical Action Publishing is a trading name of Practical Action Publishing Ltd (Company Reg. No. 1159018), the wholly owned publishing company of Practical Action. Practical Action Publishing trades only in support of its parent charity objectives and any profits are covenanted back to Practical Action (Charity Reg. No. 247257, Group VAT Registration No. 880 9924 76). Latin America Bureau (Research and Action) Limited is a UK registered charity (no. 1113039).

Since 1977 LAB has been publishing books, news, analysis and information about Latin America, reporting consistently from the perspective of the region's poor, oppressed or marginalized communities, and social movements. In 2015 LAB entered into a publishing partnership with Practical Action Publishing.

Obra publicada com o apoio da Fundação Biblioteca Nacional, do Ministério da Cultura do Brasil, e do Instituto Guimarães Rosa, do Ministério das Relações Exteriores do Brasil.

This work is published with support from the National Library Foundation of the Brazilian Ministry of Culture and the Guimarães Rosa Institute of the Brazilian Foreign Ministry.

Cover design by: Katarzyna Markowska, Practical Action Publishing
Cover illustration by: Ênio Squeff
Typeset by vPrompt eServices Pvt. Ltd.

The manufacturer's authorised representative in the EU for product safety is Lightning Source France, 1 Av. Johannes Gutenberg, 78310 Maurepas, France.
compliance@lightningsource.fr

ENGLISH
PEN

Supported using public funding by

**ARTS COUNCIL
ENGLAND**

This book has been selected to receive financial assistance from English PEN's PEN Translates programme, by Arts Council England. English PEN exists to promote literature and our understanding of it, to uphold writers' freedoms around the world, to campaign against the persecution and imprisonment of writers for stating their views, and to promote the friendly co-operation of writers and the free exchange of ideas. www.englishpen.org

We are all perplexed
awaiting a congress of the
mutilated in body and soul.

—Alex Polari, *Inventory of Scars*

They're out there somewhere
In the clouds or a grave
They're out there somewhere
Of that I'm certain
in the southern reaches of my heart

—Mario Benedetti, 'The Disappeared'

Foreword

By David Treece

For many English-speaking readers, the Portuguese or Spanish word *desaparecidos* immediately brings to mind the thousands of activists who were secretly imprisoned, abducted, and killed by the dictatorships of Latin America's Southern Cone during the 1960s, 70s and 80s. *Desaparecido/a* is sometimes translated as 'missing', but this fails woefully to capture the violence of what was at stake. As Bernardo Kucinski explains in the Afterword to this book, the *disappeared* did not randomly vanish from sight but were deliberately eliminated, as objects of a transitive verb – in other words, they were forcibly *made to disappear*. Across history disappearance has been deployed as an instrument of state repression and terror in order to punish the defeated, the condemned, and the insubordinate by violating their right to dignity in death, denying them a proper burial or funeral in an effort to erase their very existence and memory.

The use of disappearance under Brazil's 1964–85 dictatorship was recently brought to the attention of international audiences by Walter Salles's 2024 feature film *I'm Still Here*, focusing on Eunice Paiva's struggle to uncover the truth about her husband, opposition congressman Rubens

Paiva, who was arrested, tortured, and murdered in 1971 by agents of the military regime. According to the National Truth Commission's final report of 2014, a total of 243 people underwent forced disappearance during those years, that's to say more than half the fatal victims of the dictatorship's repression. But as *The Congress of the Disappeared* powerfully reveals, those official figures represent just the tip of an iceberg of disappearances perpetrated by the Brazilian state, extending over decades and centuries, as well as the legions of other disappeared across the Latin American continent and the wider world.

In Kucinski's 'prose drama', the idea of reuniting the ghosts of the disappeared is initiated, half a century on, by two deceased veterans of the underground guerrilla struggles of the 1970s. But as the gathering unfolds, they realize that it must open its doors to countless others: such as members of the Sapé Peasant League, the first casualties of the regime, and the estimated 8,300 Indigenous people who died at its hands; but also the earlier, historical victims of state repression, including those who resisted slavery in the *quilombo* strongholds and rebellions, and the activists of the eighteenth- and nineteenth-century anti-colonial and democratic movements, not to mention the disappeared of Chile, Argentina, Colombia, Guatemala, and Peru, and of Algeria, Kosovo, and Rwanda.

The congress is haunted, too, by the victims of present-day police violence and political assassination, such as Amarildo de Souza, a bricklayer from the Rocinha favela in Rio de Janeiro, who disappeared in 2013 after being called in for questioning by police officers on his way home from the market; and the community activist Marielle Franco, who was executed in March 2018 by former policemen linked to local criminal and political interests. Indeed, one of the crucial insights of *The Congress of the Disappeared* is precisely to highlight that continuity between the longer history of forced disappearance and its contemporary manifestation in Brazil. In both its past and present forms the same principle applies – 'no body, no crime'; in other words, impunity is guaranteed by the elimination of the victim's physical being. And those responsible for many of today's crimes, those whom Kucinski's characters refer to as 'the fascists', are likewise the inheritors of a long historical tradition of institutionalized violence: 'They're also the ghosts of the past: slaveowners reincarnated as businessmen, bounty hunters as bank managers, bloodthirsty despots as political demagogues.'

As Rodriguez, one of the book's key protagonists, puts it: 'A society which forgets its disappeared is condemned to a future of more disappearances.' In that sense, the fictional congress imagined by Kucinski is a rehearsal for the act of remembrance which he is effectively demanding of us, his readers, and of his country: the imperative to prevent the permanent erasure of the disappeared, to rescue them from the oblivion to which they were consigned – by taking up their demand for justice and making them heard and seen once more. More than just a commemorative ritual, the task the characters set themselves of gathering together the dispersed, lost souls of the disappeared represents, in dramatic form, the challenge of restoring their memory through a long overdue act of restorative justice.

To give this substance, a number of legal and judicial measures are needed: to revise the 1979 Amnesty Law, which absolved those military officers involved in violent acts of repression, including torture and assassination; to redefine disappearance in Brazilian law as a specific crime against humanity, by incorporating into the Penal Code the United Nations' International Convention for the Protection of All People from Enforced Disappearance (a congressional bill to this effect has been stalled at a committee stage since March 2021); to meet all twenty-nine of the recommendations of the National Truth Commission's 2014 report, only two of which had been implemented by December 2024, and to resume the work of the Special Commission on Dead and Disappeared, which was created in 1995, extinguished in late 2022 under the Bolsonaro administration and reconstituted under Lula da Silva's Presidency in July 2024.

Just as important as these measures and the demand for a proper settling of accounts with the perpetrators of political torture and disappearance, this book makes another call, to give a renewed, living status and agency to the disappeared. Or as Rodriguez puts it, to constitute the figure of a new archetype, 'the disappeared political activist'. The true horror of disappearance is that of being consigned to a kind of limbo – as dispersed ghosts in the fictional realm of Kucinski's text, and as politically orphaned and stateless beings in the real world. To bring the disappeared out of that limbo of oblivion and victimhood into the public consciousness, as this book allows us to imagine so movingly, is to give them visibility once more, to return their voice of protest to them, to make the narratives and mythologies of their struggles audible again, in short, to make them *present*. In today's Brazil, as the New Right repeatedly strives to rehabilitate the reputation of the 1964–85 dictatorship and to defend and celebrate its brutal repression of democratic liberties and rights, that task could not be more urgent.

Note to readers
Some of the less familiar names, places, and events mentioned in the text are explained briefly in the Glossary at the end of this volume.

1.

I was wandering far away, distracted, when abruptly, as if seized by some invisible yet determined hands, I felt myself pulled towards the Praça da República, which I hadn't seen since Rodriguez and I were ambushed there more than forty years ago. I came upon a city full of homeless people, beggars, children in rags. The old town was full of miserable tarpaulin shacks; it looked like a refugee camp.

The square was completely different to the way I remembered it. In my mind it had lush vegetation, it bustled with children at the end of the school day. But the school had become some drab government office. The barren trees and the patchy grass recalled an old man who had let himself go. Threadbare shapes occupied the bandstand. It was the end of a hot, airless afternoon. Some kids were paddling in the filthy waters of the lake.

I couldn't find the benches where we used to meet, pretending to be lovers. Squinting towards the far end of the square, I spotted a low wall beneath a lamppost, where I sat down and let my mind wander, my thoughts erratic, like the flight of a little bird. I reflected on what I had just seen. These people were the same down-and-outs as always, but now they had been cast aside once and for all. The new times had no need for them. Then I thought about the past and the persistence of memory. Looking out upon the present, I still felt haunted by the past.

Those had been both my best years, and my worst. We were young, and we were rebels. We all wanted to give our lives meaning, something important, perhaps heroic. We considered revolution to be our destiny. Defeat an army, change the world, anything seemed possible. How naïve! How deluded! How pathetically deluded! Once we realized we were beaten, we panicked. And still we pressed on regardless, as if goading the angel of death. I asked myself yet again, how could we have possibly believed in it? And now, with the people still mired in poverty and ignorance, and with even nature itself convulsed with disasters and epidemics that might seem to foreshadow the end of the world, what had been the point of our sacrifice?

Lost in my thoughts, I didn't realize at first that a figure had sat down next to me. Turning to look, I saw that their face was disfigured. Even so, there was something about it that rang a bell. I gazed at them, for longer this time. They had a prominent chin, a protruding jaw, almost like a deformity. I knew that jaw. They were gazing back at me too. Suddenly, they extended their hands.

'Japa!'

That was when I recognized him.

'Rodriguez!' And we embraced.

Hurriedly, we started talking over one another. Rodriguez had felt the same urge to revisit the square, at the same time. And he had sat down next to me, on the same wall.

'What a lot of coincidences,' I said.

'They're not coincidences,' he replied. 'Coincidence is random, it doesn't mean anything; I think something important to both of us must have brought us together.'

'What might that be?' I asked.

'Well, perhaps some kind of simultaneity of desires,' he suggested, 'as we both felt the same impulse at the same time.'

Later we surmised we had been brought together by the Fates – these were Rodriguez's words, he was a scholar of mythology – to give some meaning to our pointless and sterile existence.

'Perhaps for us to rebel again,' he ventured.

I then confessed that I could no longer stand the boredom and the loneliness.

'I've immersed myself in philosophy,' he said. 'I hardly had any time for it before, but now – without activism, without the daily grind, without even the need to go anywhere – I have plenty of time on my hands. It's almost like time has nowhere to go either.'

We stared at each other again in silence. A whole minute went by.

'You haven't changed a bit,' Rodriguez said eventually. 'You look so well!'

But I couldn't say the same. I asked what had happened to him.

'They beat the shit out of me,' he said, lowering his voice. 'I was shouting that our cover was blown, but you couldn't hear me.'

'I heard you, but there was no time to do anything,' I said, 'I was killed on the spot. I wasn't ready for it,' I added bitterly.

'None of us were,' said Rodriguez, 'we were afraid of torture, that's true, we were all terrified of the *pau de arara*, but nobody thought much about dying.'

'I used to think about it sometimes,' I said, 'I was scared that one or other of my comrades might die.'

'Me too,' said Rodriguez, 'but I wasn't scared of dying myself, I don't think anyone really thinks about their own death.'

I had fallen right there, close to where we were sitting. But rather than allow my parents to give me a decent burial, they made me disappear. 'I didn't even see where they took me. And you?' I asked Rodriguez. 'Where did they take you?'

'I lost count how many times they buried me and dug me up again,' he said. 'In the end they dumped me in that mass grave in the cemetery in Perus. My remains were all mixed up with the others, it was impossible to identify me.'

'They sure as hell won't identify you now,' I said, 'they wound up the National Truth Commission.'

'The families should have protested,' said Rodriguez.

'More than they already had?' I retorted. 'It's tiring, and too much time had gone by in any case.'

Rodriguez nodded. Then I had an idea that left him speechless. 'What about if *we* protest? If we got together and launched a manifesto, that would really be something!'

Rodriguez said nothing, frowning as if he hadn't understood. He remained quiet for some time, with a distant look in his eye. Suddenly he sat upright, stared at me and said, 'A meeting of the disappeared! What a brilliant idea! A national meeting of the disappeared! The dead haunting the living! Why didn't anyone think of this before?'

'We let our voice fade away,' I said. 'Others speak for us. Some of them tell lies; others think they know, but we're the only ones who understand the extreme nature of disappearance, its true horror. So it's our voice which needs to be heard, who knows, perhaps we'll shake things up a bit?'

Rodriguez nodded. 'A society which forgets its disappeared is condemned to a future of more disappearances.'

'In other countries they haven't forgotten,' I said, 'how do you explain it here?'

'Well, we had that whole outbreak of fascism,' he said, 'it was a massive setback. Where do you think the fascists came from? They didn't come out of nowhere. They're also the ghosts of the past: slaveowners reincarnated as businessmen, bounty hunters as bank managers, bloodthirsty despots as political demagogues. We must take a stand.'

As he talked, Rodriguez became more and more animated. 'How will we summon the disappeared,' he wondered, 'without access to social networks?'

'It'll have to be word of mouth,' I said.

'In that case,' said Rodriguez, 'we have to decide on the day, the time and the place right now; do you think one day will be enough?'

'Better set aside two or even three,' I said, 'we've got a lot to discuss.' I suggested the week of 1st May – a date that none of our people forget, and it would give us four months to organize things. And the place? I thought about it for a moment. The place ... the place ... eventually, I suggested the Municipal Theatre.

'It has good acoustics and it's empty from Monday to Wednesday,' I said.

But Rodriguez objected. 'Places are symbolic, and the Municipal Theatre is bourgeois, it was built by the coffee barons. Why not Sé Cathedral? It also has good acoustics, and cathedrals are transcendental places, they express majesty, as soon as you enter you feel the presence of the sacred, a sense of wonder.'

Surprised, I asked: 'I thought you were a materialist! Have you found religion?'

'No, I'm still agnostic,' he replied. 'But the sacred has its place in the human psyche. Not everything can be explained by matter, we have imagination, the magic of creation, the Bachs, the Michelangelos. There's something within us that goes beyond what is determined by society, perhaps beyond even our own physical existence. If that weren't the case, we wouldn't be here now, would we?'

This speech threw me a little; I didn't know how to respond. He continued: 'Besides which, the ecumenical mass for Vladimir Herzog was held at the cathedral. It's a place full of significance for us.'

'Let's do it in the cathedral then,' I said.

And so it was agreed. The first National Meeting of the Disappeared would come to order the night of 1st May, in Sé Cathedral.

The faces of comrades I was eager to see again came to my mind. 'It's been a while since I ran into any of our old comrades,' I said, 'how about you?'

'Same,' he said, 'I used to see Jonas hanging around the mass grave at Perus, but not for ages now.'

'The bones aren't there anymore,' I said, 'they were taken to the Centre for Anthropology and Forensic Archaeology set up by the university. There was a lot of evidence, more than 1,000 boxes.'

'I didn't know,' said Rodriguez. 'Forensic archaeology ... we've become the fossils of past eras,' he joked.

We spent the night reminiscing. Rodriguez's memory was exceptional, and he recalled things that I had forgotten. He had been the oldest of our group, by far the most well educated. While we were all still wet behind the ears, he was working on a PhD, something to do with medieval myths of the apocalypse. He had read all the Greek philosophers and a lot of mythology too, including from Africa. He would recommend us books and authors off the top of his head. He used to get carried away, and give us these long speeches, lectures really. This sometimes made us uncomfortable, though he didn't even realize; he wasn't doing it to show off. And then he surprised us all when, with his PhD nearly finished, he packed it all in and threw himself into Marxism.

Rodriguez's worldview tended more towards anarchism or perhaps even nihilism than our Leninism. 'Anarchism is libertarian, Leninism is authoritarian,' he would say.

I had a hard time understanding what drew him to the armed struggle, because he hadn't a clue how to handle a pistol. Once, when we were in hiding together for several days, I asked him to explain anarchism to me. So he gave me a lesson about the workers' uprisings in the coalmines and the first textile mills. He said that anarchism awakened the imagination of the workers, so much so that they created hundreds of newspapers and magazines and workers' associations all over the world, whereas Leninism, which came later, suffocated it. He told me he had joined the armed struggle because one of the demands of anarchism is to act, to go beyond words.

Suddenly I remembered Borges. 'You're not thinking of inviting Borges?' I asked.

'Why not?' he said.

'Well, you know what they say about him.'

'I know,' he said, 'but others swear it's not true.'

'He's a traitor,' I said, 'it's been proven.'

Rodriguez said nothing at first, and then said, 'It's rash to judge others, we tend to judge without knowing the details, and in this case we know nothing.'

'So no-one can be judged?' I asked. 'No-one is guilty?'

'We all know whether or not we're guilty,' said Rodriguez.

'Fine,' I said, 'we'll invite him, it'll be an acid test.'

'An acid test of what?' asked Rodriguez.

'Of Borges – if he doesn't turn up it's because he sold us out. The traitors shun all contact; they drift like lost souls.'

'You're not being fair,' said Rodriguez, 'did you get strung up?'

'No, but I know what it was like.'

'Well I did,' he said, 'you just want it to stop, you'd kill yourself given the chance. The worst of it is the fear, it drives some people mad. You know that.'

'Yes, I know,' I had to admit.

I felt embarrassed and fell quiet for a while. I thought of Borges, of how he must have suffered. Images came to my mind of Avaré, matinées at the cinema, his election to the student union. We only drifted apart when he decided to study medicine, while I took engineering. His betrayal had hit me like a bolt of lightning.

Rodriguez resumed his speech: 'Today we're all equal. We're all in the same boat, the same limbo, scattered through the immensity of nothingness, drifting through non-places. The meeting will make us comrades on a new journey, perhaps even a transcendental, historic one. Only those who lived the glory days of our youth can understand the scale of the tragedy today. There's nothing in our recent history so calamitous as this outbreak of fascism. It's not just that it has destroyed the environment and shredded our social fabric, but it has rotted the soul of so many Brazilians.'

So spoke Rodriguez, and he spoke well. I nodded, impressed once again by his oratory. I was reminded not just of his erudition, but of how he always managed to see the bigger picture. And so, out of this encounter – which, for Rodriguez, was no coincidence, but one orchestrated by the Fates, perhaps remorseful for the harm they had done us in the past, or shocked by what he called the outbreak of fascism – the First National Congress of the Disappeared was born.

When we parted, it was already a new day.

2.

No sooner had we gone our separate ways than doubts began to creep in. How much did we matter, really? There were so few of us, 300 if that. A small part of all the disappeared from the Southern Cone, just a tiny fraction of the disappeared from all of history. Could we, being so few, force the reckoning that Rodriguez had spoken of? In Chile and Argentina they managed it, but their disappeared were in the thousands, including people from well-known urban families. In Peru too, thousands were disappeared, but as most of them had been rural peasants, it made no difference. No Peruvian general was ever brought to justice.

I shared my misgivings with Rodriguez.

'What matters is that we try,' he said. 'Even if there are only a few of us, we still have to give it a shot.'

'But so much time has already gone by,' I objected.

'We've improved over time,' he said, 'we've built up a huge amount of knowledge and each and every one of us is important. When each of us died a future was lost. Imagine the family we might have built, the book we might have written, the song we might have composed. The possibilities were endless; that's why it's said that in each person all of humanity resides.'

'That's a nice idea,' I said.

'It's not mine, it's from the Talmud,' he explained, 'it says we are all unique because if a similar being had ever existed then we wouldn't need to. And our generation was also unique. Do you remember how one of our poets put it? We were the generation that stormed the heavens.'

'I remember,' I said. But I wasn't convinced. 'How could so few of us have any influence?'

'We might have just as much influence as the avatars,' he replied.

I knew nothing about avatars, so Rodriguez explained: 'Avatars are representations of the Hindu gods. Krishna is the most powerful, the eighth avatar of Vishnu, the god who preserves and protects the universe. He has immense powers and appears whenever humanity is threatened by some great evil.'

'And why would we have that same power?' I asked.

'Because we are ghostly,' said Rodriguez, 'and that's unsettling for society. Death demands some kind of rite, but our deaths never received one, they were neglected. Have you noticed there are no prayers for the disappeared, like there are for the dead? And did you know that in some cultures a death which doesn't receive the proper rites can create a malaise so profound it affects the whole community, as if it were an infectious disease?'

Of course, I had no idea.

'We didn't just lose our lives,' Rodriguez continued, 'we lost our right to a tomb. Did you know this right is enshrined in our constitution?'

I had to admit I hadn't a clue about that either.

'A tombstone tells society that there lies the body of someone who had a face, who left behind a father, mother, siblings, friends, maybe children. But we had none of that. We were dumped in mass graves, thrown into rivers, or just left in some hole in the forest. This was a violation of our human rights.'

'But how can the dead have any rights?'

'Those aren't my words, it's the law. It's in the Constitution, the right to an honourable image and the right to respect even after death. The Penal Code dedicates a whole chapter to crimes against the dead, one of which is the desecration of a body – you can be fined and sent to prison. It's not just the body, but ashes too. So you see the importance that society gives to the remains of the dead. Imagine then the impact of the disappearances in the Araguaia campaign. Twelve of them were young women with their whole lives ahead of them, murdered in the most cowardly fashion after they had surrendered. And some of our other comrades were people of great renown. Rubens Paiva had been a congressman. David Capistrano had fought in the International Brigades. Imagine the power of these spirits!'

'But more than fifty years have gone by,' I said. 'Who remembers any of these guys today?'

'They convey authority even to those who have no idea who they were,' Rodriguez replied.

'How come we're on the same journey as people who became communists in the 1920s?' I asked. 'We could've been their children, even their grandchildren.'

'These are conflicts which take lifetimes to resolve,' said Rodriguez, 'they span generations.'

'But this current generation doesn't seem to care much about anything,' I replied.

'It's too early to tell,' he said, 'every generation has the chance to make history, or at least to try.'

Well said, I thought again, but he still hadn't answered my question as to whether there would be enough of us. I left Rodriguez and decided to investigate.

So, how many of us were there? And who were we exactly? There are still no answers to these questions, because the very essence of disappearance is the negation of everything: of the body, the crime, the facts, and even our very existence in politics. We had been presumed dead, but as our bodies had never been found, there was still no proof. It's only in isolated cases that a death might be confirmed by a survivor or by a perpetrator seeking to assuage their guilty conscience.

On the official list there are 220 of us. But that doesn't include 100 or more peasants who may also have been disappeared, though it's possible they just ran away, terrified, and went into hiding under assumed names. And what about the Indigenous who disappeared? The National Truth Commission estimated that 8,300 Indigenous people died, many of whom were disappeared. But Rodriguez had explained that they wouldn't come to the congress, as their spirits inhabit other cosmogonies.

We would still invite all those comrades whose deaths had been registered, even though their bodies had never been identified. They didn't have a proper burial either – they were thrown into mass graves and their remains mixed with those of others. There are twenty-eight of them. That makes 248. Then at any moment someone might come forward to report a missing father, or even a grandfather, despite all the time that has passed. Yet more disappeared, who we still don't know anything about. But if the remains of any disappeared individual are identified, they'll receive a proper burial, and they'll no longer be one of us.

There are some who will never be laid to rest: the young people from the Araguaia campaign whose bodies were incinerated in the Serra das Andorinhas, as well as fourteen more who were cremated in the furnace of a sugar mill in Campos dos Goytacazes. These are the eternal disappeared. Nothing remains of them; no substance, shape, nor texture, absolutely nothing that could be put together or restored. Their ashes will never be buried and their spirits will never find peace.

Rodriguez suggested they should lead the meeting, as they had long since given up on finding their remains and could dedicate themselves fully to this new journey.

'But they were all so young,' I said, 'most of them hadn't even turned thirty, do you think they're mature enough to lead such an important meeting?'

Rodriguez didn't respond.

I thought about what he had said about the right to a proper tomb. Without some kind of headstone to invite reflection on our existence, without an epitaph to mark our passage through the world, we were trapped in a kind of limbo. Dead, we couldn't be amongst the living, but unburied, we couldn't take our place amongst the dead.

Even without identification of our remains, those responsible for our disappearance could have been put on trial for kidnapping and concealing a body. But society had been in a rush to forgive them. And if at any point people had found our ambiguous kind of existence upsetting, they soon forgot about us. That was the fatal error.

For most of us, the way we died was consistent with the way we lived. We all died very young. We knew little of life. All of us, without exception, witnessed for too long the torment of our families in the desperate search for our whereabouts, and then, for our remains. But this isn't just a story of individual misfortune. Each of us died the death of the other. Each individual life was intertwined with the lives of others, with countless groups, and even the accidental revolutionaries, attracted to the project of changing the world, and for that reason, killed and disappeared. Rodriguez was right: each one of us mattered.

The first to be disappeared were Nego Fubá and Pedro Fazendeiro, on 7th September 1964 – Independence Day – in the army barracks at João Pessoa. At this point there was no system of forced disappearance, but simply repeated acts of police brutality that needed to be covered up. Both men were leaders of the Sapé Peasant League. It would be incredible if they came to the meeting, I thought.

Four years later, they disappeared Jonas, the leader of National Liberation Action. Jonas was killed not by an individual psychopath, but by a psychopathic organization. By this point, disappearance was becoming the policy of a criminal state. The apparatus of disappearance was emerging, and a terrorist state was emerging – no longer just a military dictatorship, but a qualitative shift in the nature of power, with the state of exception becoming a permanent structure, abolishing all individual and collective rights and freedoms.

Exploiting tried and tested methods of disposing of the bodies of the poor and marginalized, more than thirty of us were given false names and buried as vagrants. Those were barbarous times. The disappearances multiplied. From 1973, the criminal state decided that anyone who secretly returned to Brazil from exile had to die. And so the militants from the Popular Liberation Movement who came back from Cuba were hunted down and shot, one by one. There are five of them among us. Then the criminal state unleashed Operation Radar, which would more accurately have been called Operation Extermination. The aim was to disappear any political leader of note whatsoever, regardless of whether or not they had taken up arms against the dictatorship.

The method, approved by the general occupying the presidential palace and the head of the secret service, replaced the whole charade of the simulated hit and runs, an inadequate strategy which was deemed to have run its course. It was decided that all political activists of any influence must be disappeared, not for anything they had done or hadn't done, but for what they were, for the influence they might have in an eventual democracy that could be glimpsed on the horizon and would need to be controlled. Disappearance became a tool with which to organize the desired social order.

The following year there were fifty-four disappearances, including a group from the Popular Revolutionary Vanguard who were tricked into returning from exile so they could be liquidated.

But our biggest contingent was a group of sixty Communist Party militants who were discovered by the army while planning a guerrilla campaign in the Amazon, then systematically hunted down and murdered. To cover it up, for decades the army simply denied the existence of any guerrilla campaign at all. In the interim, they dug up the bodies and cremated them. Although twenty-nine were subsequently found, only two of them were identified. All despots are alike. Once the Second World War began to turn against Germany, Hitler ordered that the remains of his victims be exhumed and cremated.

I've described who we were not to glorify us or to look for sympathy – the time for hero narratives is long gone – but just to ensure the record of who attended our meeting would be accurate. I showed Rodriguez the list.

'There's one missing,' he said.

'Who?'

'Amarildo. You know, the bricklayer.'

'Amarildo? He had nothing to do with us. He wasn't our comrade, he's not even from our time. And even in his own day he wasn't politically engaged at all, he was totally alienated.'

But Rodriguez disagreed: the people had made Amarildo one of our own, and his disappearance symbolized the permanence of the murderous state through time. So spoke Rodriguez, and once again I had to agree.

3.

But as it happened, we couldn't find any of our old comrades. A sad and despondent Rodriguez had fared no better than I had. We had both searched in vain – me, along the corridors of the Federal University of São Paulo; he, down the avenues of the Ricardo de Albuquerque cemetery in Rio de Janeiro, where fifteen of us lie in a mass grave. I also lingered at the Memorial to the Disappeared on the University of São Paulo campus. And nothing.

We racked our brains, perplexed. Where could they be? Rodriguez suggested that our encounter in the Praça da República had been even more significant than he had thought.

'The Fates must have some higher purpose,' he said, 'which is still unknown to us.'

'What could that be?' I asked.

'Maybe to thwart a plot by other gods sympathetic to the fascists,' he said.

'So we've become the playthings of the gods?'

'Maybe, it happens often in mythology,' Rodriguez said, citing the fight between Hector and Achilles in the Trojan Wars, when Pallas Athena helps Achilles, and Apollo and Zeus protect the Trojans.

We spent that night brooding. With the first rays of the morning light, Rodriguez had a brainwave. 'We need to discuss memory,' he said. 'We exist in the memory of the living. If we've vanished, it's either because they've died, or they've forgotten us, which amounts to the same thing. Did you know that for the Greeks being forgotten was equivalent to death?'

I didn't know, so he explained, in that donnish manner of his. 'In Greek mythology, one of the rivers of the underworld is called Lethe, a word which means forgetting. Whoever drinks or even touches the waters of Lethe forgets everything.'

'It makes sense,' I said, 'people today only know us from photos. Our parents have died, our siblings too, apart from the odd one or two who were born much later.'

'And there are some so traumatized they'll do anything to forget,' said Rodriguez.

'I'm not so sure,' I said, 'some things you never forget.'

'It's a defence mechanism,' said Rodriguez. 'The Greeks knew about this, that's why in Greek the opposite of Lethe isn't memory, which we think of as the opposite of forgetting, but truth – in other words, to forget is to flee from the truth and to remember is to accept it.'

'So they drink from the waters of Lethe to be able to live?' I asked.

'Or to stay sane,' said Rodriguez, 'they can only achieve inner peace by forgetting.'

'What about our children?' I asked, 'have they forgotten us too?'

'What children?' said Rodriguez. 'Not many of us had kids. Besides, the memories of these children are conflicted. On the one hand they admire us, they're proud of their parents, but on the other they have an unconscious resentment which stems from being abandoned, their condition as orphans.'

I pressed my point further. 'What about grandchildren? You know how strong the bond is between grandparents and their grandchildren.'

'I don't,' Rodriguez said, 'I didn't have any, I didn't even have time for children.'

'Well I had a grandson,' I said, 'it's a bond which is intimate, yet simple, without all the responsibilities of parenthood.'

'But any grandparents among us can't have spent much time with their grandchildren,' said Rodriguez. 'So what the grandchild remembers are false memories, based mostly on what they've heard. That type of memory doesn't count. Look, the fact of the matter is that everyone has vanished. That demands an explanation, and the only one I can think of is this: if we exist in the memories of others and no-one has shown up, it's because we've been forgotten and therefore, we no longer exist.'

'Wow. We no longer exist?' – this I couldn't accept. 'What about the comrades who survived?' I asked. 'Have they forgotten us as well?'

'They're probably feeling guilty,' said Rodriguez, 'and will do anything to forget.'

'Guilty? Guilty about what?'

'Guilty for having survived,' he said. 'You know you don't need to have been blamed for something to feel guilt.'

That was true, but I wasn't giving in. 'If I'm present in the memory of even one of my comrades, then I still exist,' I said. 'And the two of us are here now, aren't we? So I exist in you, and you in me.'

That took him by surprise. He didn't know what to say and spent some time in quiet reflection. Finally, he conceded that my reasoning made sense. 'It must be because our bonds are strong and theirs aren't,' he said. 'If someone supresses people from their memory it's because the emotional bond between them has broken.'

But I didn't like this explanation either. 'Even if all our family members have died, and even if all our friends and comrades have forgotten us, we also exist in memorials, like those at the Ricardo de Albuquerque cemetery, the University of São Paulo campus, and Xambioá in the Amazon, close to where the Araguaia campaign unfolded.'

'But the fascists have torn most of them down,' said Rodriguez, 'and even if any are still standing, they're just matter, they don't think, they have no feelings or memory.'

'That sounds paradoxical,' I said, 'memorials without memory.'

'They're just symbols,' he said. 'What matters is living memory, with the ability to reinterpret things, stone can't do that.'

'What about Google?' I asked. 'We're in the cloud and Google never forgets.'

'That's true,' said Rodriguez, 'but if no-one accesses any material on us then it counts for nothing.'

'Well, maybe that's why the Fates have orchestrated our meeting,' I said. 'It's to prevent our permanent erasure.'

Rodriguez looked at me, stunned. 'My gosh, I think you've nailed it!'

4.

Two weeks had gone by since my initial meeting with Rodriguez. The Ides of March came around, carnival time. The streets filled with girls and boys swigging beer from the can, practically oozing sex. There were none of the elaborate costumes people had worn in the past, just plastic tat made in China. And there were no sharp, socially critical *marchinhas* to be heard anywhere; it was a constant racket.

'It's the carnival of a lost generation,' said Rodriguez, 'they're not even really celebrating, just faking it.'

We began to fear that the congress would be a failure. The suspicion was growing that we had indeed been erased from the collective memory. And it hurt.

But we were wrong. At the very climax of the carnival, the Mangueira samba school – of all the issues it could have chosen to address – made *us* the protagonists of its *samba-enredo*. They paid us tribute in a spectacular parade, alongside famous rebels who had fought oppression throughout history. Their performance, entitled *Bedtime Stories for Grown-ups*, celebrated the Brazil of the oppressed and its heroes: from the Indigenous who were massacred by the Portuguese colonizers to the Black city councillor Marielle Franco, murdered five centuries later.

'This is all thanks to Marielle,' I said. 'Her face is all over Rio de Janeiro and her killing was covered everywhere online. People are furious no-one has been brought to justice.'

'Marielle wasn't just a successful councillor,' Rodriguez added, 'but a Black woman from a favela, a single mother, a lesbian, an activist. She embodied all these things, and that's why she was killed. This is what I mean by living memory; they've gone delving into history looking for clues to a crime which happened today.'

The parade celebrated leaders of the popular resistance and poured scorn on their murderers. In the grandstands, the crowds were going wild. Stunned, we heard verses which spoke directly of our experience:

> *'They are crosses without names, without bodies, without dates, memories of a time when to fight for your rights was a death sentence.'*

It was unbelievable; it was as if they knew of our dejection and were saying: 'Don't give up.'

On a pedestal, on a float led by dozens of dancers, stood Hildegard Angel, imposing as a goddess. She was sister of our comrade Tuti, who had been murdered and disappeared. All dressed in black, with dark sunglasses, she was the embodiment of grief. Behind her was a photo of the words 'Murdering Dictatorship', graffitied onto a wall in enormous letters, with soldiers in their helmets blurred and distorted below it. The black-and-white tones of the image contrasted with the brilliant colours of the parade.

Young Black girls held up great effigies of Marielle. A girl up on the shoulders of one of the dancers displayed a banner reading 'Viva Marielle'. Pedro Álvares Cabral was portrayed as a brutal colonizer and a petty dealer in trinkets; the *bandeirantes*, the explorers who killed and enslaved the Indigenous, were represented by skulls dripping with blood. This was all followed by hundreds of dancers waving flags with Marielle's image.

Then there appeared an enormous Brazilian flag, transformed into a banner of protest. The background was purple rather than green, paying tribute to women, and in the band across the circle, the usual motto 'Order and Progress' had been replaced by the words 'Indian, Black, and Poor'.

There were people dressed in costumes honouring those who had fought oppression. Ganga Zumba, Zumbi dos Palmares, Tiradentes. The Malê slaves, who rose up time and time again in Bahia and who were crushed ruthlessly, were represented by hundreds of figures in African masks and pointed helmets, brandishing long spears with sharp heads. They were followed by the Guarani Indians, wearing brilliant blue head-dresses. The climax of the show came with the appearance of the Bahian women, hundreds of them, swirling around in their lace skirts and colourful jewellery.

At my side, Rodriguez watched it all go by, every bit as fascinated as I was. 'Beautiful, just beautiful,' he said at the end of the parade, clearly emotional. 'Carnival is a celebration of mockery, but this was a serious protest, an angry protest, without irony or sarcasm. What most impressed me was how they associated the impunity of Marielle's murder with the impunity of our disappearance. They situated what happened to Marielle in a broader context which gives it meaning. This means we're absolutely a part of the collective memory of Mangueira.'

'Just of Mangueira,' I asked, 'or of the people as a whole?'

Rodriguez shook his head. 'If it were the people as a whole, then the whole outbreak of fascism would never have happened.'

I was quiet for a moment. Then I said, slowly, but with conviction, 'If carnival is a popular celebration, and if we exist in the collective memory of Mangueira, then the congress will go ahead.'

'For sure,' said Rodriguez, 'it has to, we just need to find the others. Where can they have got to?'

'I don't know,' I said, 'they might be wandering out in the non-places or resting on distant clouds online.'

'Wherever they are,' said Rodriguez, 'after a parade like that, I'm sure they'll show up. After Ash Wednesday we'll have another look for them, and this time we'll expand the search.'

And that's exactly what we did.

5.

The parade took place on Saturday. On Monday, we met in the square. Rodriguez was euphoric.

'You'll never guess who I found,' he said, 'Pedro Tim!'

'No way!' I said. 'Where?'

'In the cathedral, I went to check what time they were holding mass and there he was, huddled up in a side chapel.'

'Pedro Tim was in the cathedral?' I asked. 'But his family wasn't Catholic, they were Lutheran.'

'Presbyterian,' Rodriguez corrected me, 'I did ask him if he had converted to Catholicism and he said he wasn't praying, but meditating. He said after he was disappeared he found he needed somewhere to think and the cathedral was the best place.'

'His parents were Canadian,' I said, 'why didn't he take refuge in the Canadian Embassy once everything fell apart?'

'I asked him that,' said Rodriguez. 'He's been asking himself the same thing. For a while he thought it was out of bravery, then he thought that he had been drawn to martyrdom, then finally he decided it was out of guilt for those who had fallen, though he swears he was never remiss about the security protocols.'

'And what does he say about the armed struggle?' I asked.

'He has some doubts, and the more he thinks about it, the more doubts he has. But there's one thing he's sure about: it wasn't a rational political choice, in fact it wasn't a choice at all, it was what was demanded by the times, sort of like fate.'

'And do you agree?' I asked.

'Yes, for the most part. It wasn't a rational political decision, not at the beginning, and even less so after Marighella's murder.'

'What else did Pedro Tim say?' I asked.

'He said that ever since he was a child he had had a religious imagination, he believed in life after death, then when he was a teenager he did some volunteering, trying to find a truly selfless way of life. He talked a lot about that, he said that Christianity has always had two sides to it. One is gentle, based on the imperative to love one another and on the figure of Christ; the other pre-dates Christ and is condescending, millennialist, seeking the redemption of the poor and the victims of injustice. So when he and his comrades swapped Jesus for Marx, the gentleness gave way to revolutionary violence. But he's always hated violence; he said it would be better if nobody had to die for their beliefs. It was like he was confessing. He sounded melancholy, I think he might be depressed.'

'And what about us?' I asked Rodriguez. 'We don't have a religious bone in our body, so in hindsight, what do you think motivated us?'

'Revolutionary reason,' Rodriguez replied brusquely. 'We were compelled by revolutionary reason!'

'Ah, so it was rational,' I said. 'A minute ago you said it wasn't. So which is it to be?'

Rodriguez seemed surprised by this, and a few seconds went by. 'The rationality was moral rather than political,' he replied. 'It was subjective – a belief, not an ideology.'

'I don't see the difference,' I said.

'The difference is that belief implies a certainty in achieving a goal through action. With ideology that's not always the case. That's what *foco* theory was about, the belief that action would create the conditions for the revolution, don't you remember?'

'For me it was ideology, not belief,' I said.

'Both ideology and belief come from the imagination,' said Rodriguez, 'but ideology only becomes action if there is also belief. That's why so many popular uprisings have a kind of messianic dimension to them.'

I felt ignorant. Rodriguez must have noticed my discomfort, because he quickly added: 'The fact is that our generation was predestined to act, as Pedro Tim says. Why do you think I like mythology so much? It's because in mythology humans think they're the ones calling the shots, but they're not – their fate has already been decided by the gods.'

'I've always thought we each create our own destiny,' I said.

'We do, and we don't,' said Rodriguez. 'Free will exists. Pedro Tim could have sought refuge in the Canadian Embassy, but he chose not to. We all thought about whether to fight or not, whether to stand our ground or flee. We weighed up the pros and cons and made our decision according to our will. But that decision occurred within a pre-existing social imaginary.'

'Is that what you mean by fate?' I asked.

'They're similar,' said Rodriguez. 'In sociology, a social imaginary conditions what may or may not happen, according to what has gone before, while fate is a cultural concept and is absolute – it's inevitable. In Greek mythology fate is prophesied by the Pythia and the oracles, in Yoruba mythology by the Babalawos, and in Candomblé by the *pais-de-santo*. They foresee what's going to happen and they're always right, however much you might struggle against it, and even if other unexpected things happen.'

'And what does that have to do with us?' I asked.

We were sitting on the wall. Rodriguez stood up and began a long speech, slowly and in a solemn tone, as if he were giving a lecture. What he said left me lost for words.

'The story of our generation was determined long before we were born. It was determined by the steam engine, by the relentless exploitation of the workers in the first factories, by the fourteen-hour working day. This gave rise to the anarchists, in a real explosion of rebellion and inconformity, and soon afterwards came Marx, who gave it all meaning and called for action. He was our messiah, a Moses who saw the suffering of the people and called on us to change the world order. For Marx, the people were the proletariat, and force the midwife of history, do you remember that phrase? Our struggle was to be the final battle which would lead to a new world, like in that verse from *The Internationale*, which we used to sing on 1st May. A new world and a classless society, nothing less!

'This was a powerful idea, and we made it our life project because we thought it was possible. But we were wrong. It was unattainable. It was just another creation myth, but couched in modern, rational, and philosophical terms which we found appealing, seductive. We created a whole cosmogony: mode of production, class struggle, alienation, dialectic, surplus value, historical materialism. These concepts have huge power, almost like divine revelation in religion. All of a sudden it was as if everything made sense, and the revolution was inevitable.

'But it was a fantasy. Just because we believe in the revolution, that doesn't make it possible. Faith, belief, ideology, or whatever else that might derive from our imagination don't, by themselves, create the conditions for the fulfilment of our wishes. On the contrary, they can often make it even less likely. The conditions are determined by the facts, the circumstances of each moment, and we threw ourselves into the struggle right at the time of the Economic Miracle, isolated from the population, a handful of students up against an army of 200,000 soldiers. In our cosmogony, history was on our side. But it wasn't true then, and today even less so, because the proletariat in our conception of the world is only relevant for the world in which it was created. And that world no longer exists.'

So spoke Rodriguez, and when he had finished, he sat back down on the wall. Stunned by this latest speech, I didn't know what to say.

After a few seconds, noticing my unease, he began again in a softer, almost intimate tone: 'That's why our congress won't be like any other. It'll be a reunion with a time which for us was sacred, because it was a time which formed our vision of the world, the time of a militancy that sprang from passion.'

That's more like it, I thought. 'Did you tell Pedro Tim about the meeting?' I asked.

'I did. At first he didn't understand. But when he did get his head around it, he wasn't that keen.'

'What else did he say?' I asked.

'He talked a lot about his brother, the last time they saw each other was here in this square, did you know that?'

'No I didn't. And how did they disappear Pedro Tim?'

'He said they took him out to some warehouse and beat him senseless, they didn't even bother asking many questions.'

'Why didn't he come with you?'

'He didn't want to. I did ask him, I insisted, but he said that he's not ready. He said the outbreak of fascism has plunged many into depression, including him; he said he doesn't want to see anyone. They all just want somewhere to hide away.'

I thought about this for a moment. 'No-one wants to see anyone else? So are we giving up?'

'Under no circumstances,' said Rodriguez, 'I don't want to hear another word about giving up. We'll find them somehow. Let's go to the Araguaia memorial in Xambioá, quite a few of our people are there.'

'The memorial has been abandoned,' I said.

'It doesn't matter, the Araguaia campaign has its own dimension,' he said. 'Do you know why they chose Bico do Papagaio, in the Amazon?'

'For strategic reasons,' I replied. 'Isn't it obvious?'

Rodriguez said nothing at first. Then he said, 'I think the true reason was the symbolism of the forest. The mighty Amazon was to be the birthplace of the protracted people's war, which was to be every bit as mighty.'

'That seems to be no different from what you were saying about us,' I said, 'about us having created a cosmogony.'

'The difference,' said Rodriguez, 'is that ours was conceptual, pure thought, like an abstract painting, whereas theirs was concrete, it had a territory. That makes a huge difference; by occupying the territory they consecrated it. Did you know that when João Amazonas died, thirty years after the campaign, that's where they scattered his ashes? And that even today his comrades refer to Araguaia as holy ground?'

I did. 'There's even a documentary with that name,' I said, *'Araguaia, Holy Ground.'*

'Their awareness of this holy dimension was such that they didn't associate with other groups,' said Rodriguez. 'They even had a dialect, with its own set of rules. So I don't think the disappeared of the Araguaia campaign can have succumbed to depression, and there are sixty of them.'

6.

Xambioá. I arrived late in the afternoon one Saturday, and was struck by the houses, painted in intense, contrasting colours. Just like the Indigenous who paint themselves so as not to be confused with animals, Xambioá wants to stand out from the dense forest surrounding it, I thought to myself. Looking out over the town I counted five evangelical churches. This is deep Brazil, which pays its tithes on the one hand and votes for fascists on the other, I reflected dryly.

The River Araguaia was a torrent of muddy water. Along the promenade strolled girls with painted lips and young men with hard part haircuts in the latest fashion. They exchanged glances, though without diverting much attention from their phones. At one end of the promenade, in front of some cheap hotels, there were some other girls with even more brightly painted lips. They were sitting on plastic chairs, waiting for some punters to show up.

I wondered if these kids knew anything about the Years of Lead and the guerrilla campaign. Perhaps when they were small they had heard talk of a giant named Osvaldão, who was invincible, or of a fighter called

Mariadina, who cured the sick and helped deliver babies. Just two more local myths, like the ones about the river dolphin and the giant snake. Or perhaps they had never heard of them at all.

When our young comrades travelled there in secret to meet their deaths, Xambioá was little more than a handful of wooden shacks and mud huts with straw roofs, sitting on the Goiás side of the River Araguaia. This vast region between the Araguaia and Tocantins rivers, known as Bico do Papagaio, was sparsely inhabited. Most of the locals were migrants from the northeast who were virtually illiterate. They made a living from cassava and corn; the odd pig, fish, or giant tortoise; and Brazil nuts, which they traded for salt, sugar, and coffee. Or they would sell their labour to the loggers or cattle ranchers for a plate of food. It was a place of poverty. A place without law, or government. A place of landgrabbers and guns for hire. And for the sexagenarian leaders of the Communist Party of Brazil, the ideal place to begin a protracted people's war. Afterwards, when we saw the names and ages of those who had been disappeared in the guerrilla campaign, we were shocked. Few of them were older than thirty, and some had barely even come of age.

The protracted people's war had been meticulously planned for years and was top secret, even within the party. So much so that normal party activities in the regions nearby had been suspended – the very opposite of what is required for a popular uprising.

The project was called the 'Fifth Task', and the chosen location the 'Priority Area'. Everything was in code. Most of the budding guerrillas were young people from the student movement, who had been singled out and sent to Araguaia one by one or in pairs, many women amongst them. They pretended to be settlers, hunters, artisanal miners. It was all a front. One of them opened a shop; another, a doctor who had recently finished his training, set up a small hospital and became known as Doctor Juca – a pseudonym, of course. They called this phase 'settlement'. There was no rush. They were planting the seeds for the long term. Six years went by like this.

But from the very beginning, the army had a file on them. The party top brass knew this, because not long after the first guerrillas arrived in Araguaia, there was a big front-page scoop in the *Folha de S. Paulo* about communist militants training in China to prepare for a guerrilla campaign in Brazil. It was a long, elaborate report, published over two days, containing the names and photos of many of those involved. The only thing missing was the location of where exactly the campaign was to take place, though it included a map of Brazil with areas highlighted in Mato Grosso, Goiás, and Pernambuco. The plan had been discovered by the Americans when they picked up some of the militants in transit through Karachi, on their way to China.

In 1971, the army began the search, launching Operation Mesopotamia in the south of the Amazon. They identified Juca, one of those who had been photographed in Karachi, in Porto Franco, and disseminated posters with photos of the guerrillas, whom they called terrorists. The following year, they attacked. They had discovered the exact location of the group, in Igarapé dos Caianos, through the torture of one militant who had abandoned the campaign. The torture methods which became routine in Brazil during this period were unimaginable, even for grizzled veterans who had survived the horrors of the Estado Novo dictatorship. In six months, eleven of the militants were dead, including Juca, the only doctor, and Fátima, alias Preta, who had been renowned as a fighter ever since her student days.

In September of that year, the army withdrew, no doubt planning to return with even greater firepower. Now that the guerrillas' cover had been blown, defeat was inevitable. Yet the army didn't come back for a year – more than enough time to organize a safe and orderly withdrawal. But this order was never given. In fact, the commander in charge of the campaign asked for reinforcements, 'good fighters, physically strong, and ideologically prepared to make any sacrifice necessary.' A year and a half later, having been scattered into small groups and totally isolated from one another, they would all be dead.

Rodriguez is right, I thought. Without them our congress makes no sense. I wanted to know how it all unfolded, and whether it was true or a lie spread by the army that one of the militants, Mundico, had been executed by his own comrades; and whether six others collaborated in return for their freedom and were still alive, living under new identities. If just one of the six comes to the meeting, I thought to myself, that proves it was all a lie.

I found the memorial to the campaign on the way into town, abandoned in some scrubland. The building – rectangular, unfinished – looked like a bunker. Next to it there was a satellite dish and a tall obelisk pointing skywards, painted the colour of blood. I guessed it was around eighty metres high. It seemed to express a sense of anguish before the unattainable.

Engraved on a plaque embedded in the base of the obelisk I counted fifty-nine names, and an epigraph reading 'on my body I show the marks of my time'. It reminded me of a protest song from my youth, a tough, poignant song which talked of despair, of hunger, of a lost generation, of a living death.

Suddenly I became aware of a presence. I turned round, and there was a very tall Black man, of perhaps six foot five or six. He had prominent cheekbones, thick eyebrows, close-set eyes, and a wispy little beard. His skin was intensely dark, a sign of his direct African lineage. He was barefoot, wearing just a T-shirt and shorts. His feet were enormous. I noticed he had cuts on his shins.

He smiled at me. 'It's been this way for more than ten years,' he said, pointing at the unfinished memorial. 'It's a shame, it was going to have an auditorium with a cinema, an exhibition space, a library, and a museum of the guerrilla campaign. The blue house has been left to rot as well.'

'What's the blue house?' I asked.

'It was where they tortured people in Marabá. Zezinho managed to get it protected status, but it's been abandoned just like this here.'

'Who's Zezinho?'

'He's one of the survivors. His real name is Micheas, but everyone knew him as Zezinho. He never gives up hope, but it's a waste of time, no-one is interested, not the mayor, not the governor, and as for the federal government ...'

'And how did Zezinho manage to survive?'

'He looks just like one of the locals and so he was always the one responsible for guiding comrades through the forest, he knew all the routes like the back of his hand. When it was clear the campaign had failed and the few remaining survivors were being hunted down one by one, Zezinho and Joaquim managed to escape. They only travelled at night, across the south of Pará and Goiás. When they reached Piauí they got on a bus to São Paulo, where Zezinho disappeared; he spent twenty years in hiding under an assumed name, he only reappeared after the amnesty.'

As he talked, I suddenly remembered my mission.

'You're Osvaldão! Being so tall it must be you. I came here looking for you.'

'Well you've found me,' he said, smiling. 'And who are you?'

'I'm Japa, from National Liberation Action.'

He said he didn't know much about us.

'And what happened to you?' I asked him. 'You look like a skeleton!'

'Hunger, comrade. They were looking for me and so I had to lie low; I lived on palm hearts, babassu nuts, Brazil nuts. Sometimes I'd steal a corn on the cob or kill myself a tortoise, but I didn't even have matches to light a fire, and I only had a machete to defend myself.'

'How long did that last?'

'I lost track of time; I think it was more than two months. The one leading the patrol was Arlindo Piauí, who had pretended to be my friend. I took a bullet from his rifle and fell. The last thing I saw was the lieutenant aiming at my head with a pistol. Then nothing.'

'They say you're invincible!'

'It's just a legend. They also say that I became a werewolf, and that I only died after they cut my head off. None of it is true. They did that to some of the others, they cut off arms, legs, thumbs, plenty of heads, but not mine. I died intact, as I am now. People say they buried me in the military base in Xambioá, then dug me up and burned my body in the Serra das Andorinhas. That could be true, I don't know. I know they killed a lot of local men just because they'd been my friends.'

'People also say that they flew over some of the local villages with your body hanging from a helicopter.'

'I don't know about that. Like I said, after the shot from the pistol I didn't see anything else. I know they did that to Jorge, so I guess they might have done the same to me. But why did you say you're looking for me?'

I told him about my meeting with Rodriguez, the idea of the congress and how difficult it had been to find people. As the guerrillas from Araguaia were the biggest contingent, we'd decided to see who we could find there, at the Xambioá memorial. He frowned, scratching his beard with a perplexed look about him.

'It's not going to be easy at all.'

'Why?'

'They've vanished,' he said. 'Each one is harder to find than the next.'

'But why?'

'Some because of what's going on at the moment. Having given their lives for a better Brazil, look at where we are now – the fascists have taken over. For others it's because of how they were hunted down, like animals. It was tragic; you might say they were dead before they actually died. Juca and Mariadina I see now and then, and I used to see Preta as well, but I've never seen any of the others.'

'Something that I don't understand,' I said, 'is that if the army already knew about the plan, why did you all come here? Wouldn't it have been better to back out? To make a new plan?'

'It was an order from the party and orders from the party were not to be questioned, were they? The party sent me to Czechoslovakia and so I went; they sent me here and I came. And it was the same for the others. We as individuals didn't decide; it was the party who gave the order. The party was an institution and its word was sacred. Even when there was debate about the best course of action, once an order had been given, we obeyed.'

'We have to find the others,' I insisted, 'without you lot the congress is pointless, your voice has to be heard. And it's a chance to put an end to the lies spread by the army, show people what really happened.'

My argument convinced him.

'Once again I'm the pioneer,' he said, with a little irony. 'The first time it was to help people get settled, now it's to coax them out of their hiding places.'

And just as he had appeared out of nowhere, in an instant, he disappeared.

7.

It had been eleven weeks since that promising first encounter with Rodriguez at the Praça da República. On the night of 1st May, when the final mass was over, I went to the cathedral atrium to meet Osvaldão and Pedro Tim, who had emerged from his long period of isolation.

'I finally made the decision,' he said. 'It's paradoxical: when I was alive the party decided for me; there was no "I", it was only "We". It wasn't until I was disappeared that I learned how to decide.'

'So have you come to regret your militancy?' I asked.

'Not at all,' said Pedro Tim. 'I've thought a lot about this, and I've come to the conclusion that I wasn't deluding myself. Just the opposite in fact: it was the most conscious, significant aspect of my life story, and I have to stay true to it.'

Pedro Tim had suggested that the theme for the opening session of the congress should be disappearance as a method of extermination. We had asked Rodriguez to lead, by far the most qualified for such a task, and he had stayed inside the cathedral, working on his speech. I was nervous. How many would turn up? And with how much goodwill? And what about the youngsters from the Araguaia campaign? Osvaldão said that he and Preta had managed to track down many of their comrades.

'They'll be here,' he promised.

Pedro Tim was euphoric. 'There's never been a meeting of the disappeared,' he said, 'none of the great religions have ever done this, despite their concern for the soul. We'll be the first, the pioneers. And perhaps others will follow our example, the disappeared from Algeria, Kosovo, Rwanda ...'

'And the disappeared from Chile and Argentina,' I cut in.

'Yes,' said Pedro Tim, 'and from Colombia, Guatemala, Peru, and all the other countries where we were disappeared. Have you thought about a congress of the disappeared from all Latin America?'

Osvaldão said he wanted to expose what had really happened during the Araguaia campaign.

'This is no place to air our dirty laundry though,' warned Pedro Tim. 'The congress mustn't turn into a confessional or a wailing wall. If someone needs to get things off their chest they may, but the aim should be to settle scores with the fascists.'

I realized Pedro Tim already had a clear idea of the philosophy of the meeting.

'I know there will be some tears,' he said, 'but it'll also be a happy, joyous occasion. The congress will make us active protagonists again. It'll show that you can kill the rebels, but the rebel spirit doesn't die.'

'And we're going to put an end to this image of naïve victims,' said Osvaldão.

'That's right,' said Pedro Tim. 'It was natural that our families clung to this idea while they were still looking for us, but this is about learning from the defeats of the past to fight the injustices of the present. That's what will bring out of hiding those who are still depressed.'

'And if it doesn't go well,' I asked Pedro Tim, 'and everyone ends up fighting?'

'That won't be an issue,' he said. 'It'll be fine, when the body dies, so does resentment.'

'That's not what the spiritists say,' I said.

'What they say is that with each reincarnation the spirit perfects itself, which is almost the same thing.'

I agreed, a little reluctantly. Pedro Tim continued:

'What matters is that we were comrades on a special journey, one with altruistic objectives. That's not insignificant; it makes us superior spirits, benevolent, above quarrelling and trivial matters.'

I remembered Borges' betrayal and what Rodriguez had said about judging others. 'What about those who betrayed us? Are they benevolent spirits too?' I asked.

'If they talked without having been put under duress then they're inferior spirits, and they won't come because they don't inhabit our spiritual world. What's going to happen is something very different,' said Pedro Tim mysteriously.

I asked what this something different would be, but just then the first of the disappeared began to emerge at the top of the stairs, and he didn't respond.

They came gradually, most of them alone, just as they had been during the times of clandestinity. They looked shocked by surroundings they were unused to, by the scenes of misery and destitution which had shocked me too, particularly striking there in the cathedral square, and at the foot of the stairs. They looked as if they had just awoken from a deep sleep. Those who had been killed in massacres arrived together, in groups.

They came from all corners of the country. From the Northeast came the disappeared from the Peasant Leagues, from the North the young combatants from the Araguaia campaign, from the Southeast the comrades from National Liberation Action, and from the South the soldiers from the regiment who had joined the Popular Revolutionary Vanguard, as well as six from Onofre Pinto's group who had been killed in Iguaçu National Park.

Onofre led them; he had the same prominent forehead and lofty gaze as he had back in the day. Some of the most well-known came from Rio: Rubens, Tuti, and the leaders of the party, David and Roman.

At last the Brazil of the disappeared revealed itself.

The invitation had resonated equally with those from the various political factions of that time, I thought to myself. As Pedro Tim had predicted, the tragedy had brought us together, our differences were set aside.

David, from the party, was the first to arrive. He was finely turned out in an understated suit of blue cashmere, with sharp creases and a striped tie. He looked to be intact, without any sign of mutilation. I knew what had happened to him, so complimented him on his appearance, surprised.

'I was already dead by that point,' he said, 'they did all that to me afterwards.'

He didn't enter, but stood with us to receive the others, clearly emotional. Then a dark-skinned girl arrived; with her oval face and delicate nose, she looked a little like a doll, were it not for her intense, penetrating gaze. 'This is Fátima,' said Osvaldão, 'she was among the first of the twelve women disappeared in Araguaia. She was ambushed by a military patrol and carried on fighting even after taking a bullet in the leg.'

The two of them spent some time in conversation.

Then Jonas arrived, limping. He had a compact face with deep-set eyes and had been beaten up quite badly. He greeted us one by one, stopping first in front of David and then for longer in front of Osvaldão, whom he only knew of by name. By way of explanation for his appearance, he said that once he had been detained he immediately started to goad his kidnappers.

'I knew too much,' he said, 'I couldn't risk being tortured.'

The younger ones passed by quietly, greeting us with just a look and a nod of the head; some of those who had been badly beaten moved like sleepwalkers, their gazes fixed on some invisible horizon. The older ones would stare at our little group, and when they recognized someone, would come over and give them a hug, overcome with joy. Everyone made their entrance with great solemnity, as if possessed by some great emotion.

Then two lads came bounding up the stairs. When they recognized Pedro Tim, they threw their arms around him, unable to contain their enthusiasm. They chatted for a while. I recognized them from photographs; they were Eduardo and Fernando, inseparable friends who had disappeared in Rio one Saturday during carnival. Then there appeared a very tall, skinny young man, almost skeletal, but with broad shoulders and long arms. He had a narrow face, an aquiline nose, and a melancholy expression. He came up the stairs slowly, one step at a time, constantly pushing his long, straight hair out of his face.

'That's Simão,' whispered Osvaldão, 'I didn't think he would come.' The two of them embraced for some time.

Osvaldão and Fátima introduced us to the whole cell from Araguaia, whom Pedro Tim and I had only known from hearsay. They gave their name, codename, and a few words about how each of them had been disappeared. After Simão came Sônia, an attractive woman with full lips. When she saw Osvaldão she broke into a smile, and the two of them hugged. 'She took two bullets in the leg before the fatal shot came,' Osvaldão told me afterwards. 'Then they dumped her body in the forest.' Mariadina was next to appear. A woman of an austere countenance and a serious gaze, she too was all smiles when she saw Osvaldão.

'She fought against five soldiers,' he said. 'She endured six days of torture, and died spitting in the face of her killer.'

Then came Juca, the doctor from the campaign, and Dina, who had been tortured for two weeks and then executed as she stared down her killer. Both of them hugged Osvaldão.

After a few minutes, three figures appeared at the top of the stairs. One was an olive-skinned old man, with a long face and greying hair. He was flanked by two younger men.

'That's Old Mário,' said Osvaldão, 'and the ones helping him are Olímpio and Lund.' The old man had a sleepy gaze and an impenetrable look about him.

'The three of them were shot in the Christmas Massacre of '73,' explained Osvaldão.

Zé Carlos, Old Mário's son, followed a few steps behind. David knew the older ones, all of them party veterans, and greeted Old Mário effusively. Another elderly man arrived, holding hands with a young lad of similar appearance. He must have been at least sixty; his companion, around twenty.

'Porfirio!' exclaimed David. 'How long has it been?'

'This is my son, Durvalino,' said the older man. 'He's always with me because of what happened.'

The old man and David embraced silently for a long time. Then father and son went into the cathedral. David told me their story later on. The military couldn't find Porfirio, so they arrested Durvalino, hoping he would reveal his father's hiding place. The abuse he suffered was such that he lost his mind and had to be put into a mental asylum. In the end they were both disappeared. Porfirio had six children with his first wife and twelve with his second.

'He's a character,' said David.

8.

It was the first night of the National Congress of the Disappeared. One-hundred and twenty of us were present for the opening session, though I noticed Amarildo the bricklayer hadn't shown up. People stood around in circles, talking in whispers. Raised voices were heard from time to time, though they were quickly lowered. Was this just force of habit from the times of clandestinity, or was it because they were all still in shock? I wondered. The atmosphere was reverential, a sense of mystery in the air. Rodriguez had been right. It had to be in a cathedral. And he had been right to let David preside over the meeting. He was a veteran of the struggle against fascism: in his youth he had joined the International Brigades to fight General Franco, and then the French Resistance against German occupation.

David ascended the pulpit and waited a few moments for silence, only then opening the congress.

'Comrades, welcome! So here we are, the disappeared of Brazil, and with us, in spirit, all of those who fought for a better world and were disappeared as a consequence. Too much time has gone by. The calls for justice and the identification of our remains can scarcely be heard any longer. But they remain necessary. The new fascism would never have arisen had our killers been punished. If the living have failed, then from now on it's down to us to demand truth and justice.'

He paused, as if weighing up the effect of his words. But there was no reaction. The silence was absolute. He let a whole minute go by before speaking again.

'Comrades, this being the first ever congress of the disappeared, for this opening session we have chosen as our theme the method of disappearance itself, a method which plunged our families into unimaginable torment. For this task, I call on comrade Rodriguez to speak. There will be time later for discussion, so please, no interruptions.'

Rodriguez ascended the pulpit, his prominent jaw giving him a severe look. His slow, deliberate voice echoed out into the vastness of the central nave.

'Comrades, since the dawn of history, human beings have depended on funeral rites to reconcile themselves to death. The neanderthals covered their dead with stones, to prevent the vultures from picking at the flesh. Burial became the first symbol of human existence. It has been this way for millennia and remains so today. There is no human culture without a ritual for disposing of its dead.

'The dead body is so sacred it inspired *Antigone*, one of the most powerful myths of antiquity. Creon, King of Thebes, rules that the body of the traitor Polynices must not be buried, but left to rot. Antigone, Polynices' sister, argues that the right to burial is a divine law, and covers her brother's body with earth. Creon punishes Antigone, locking her in a tomb and leaving her to starve to death. His son Haemon, who is engaged to Antigone, tries to save her, but fails. He finds her only once she has hanged herself, and kills himself too. What this myth teaches us is that denying burial to the dead is an extreme form of punishment. In battle, it was a form of taking revenge, of humiliating the enemy. That's what they did to us in Araguaia.

'In the *Iliad*, after being mortally wounded by Achilles, Hector begs for his body to be returned to Troy for burial, promising a ransom of gold and bronze in exchange. In modern times, elderly Australians travelled to Turkey to look for the remains of their sons who disappeared in the Gallipoli Campaign of the Great War; later, elderly Japanese searched the islands of the Pacific for their children who disappeared during the Second World War. In Spain, they're using radar and metal detectors to find the remains of those who were disappeared by Franco's fascists nearly a century ago.

'Why do we feel such a vital need to bury the dead? It's so their spirit can rest. In Japan, every day they put out a symbolic portion of rice for a loved one who has passed away, so their spirit can be in peace on the other side. In Chile, the Mapuches believe that if they don't keep watch over the dead body, the soul may be captured by sorcerers. The rites vary, but they all attest to the sacredness of the dead body, something which truly distinguishes us as a species.

'In the ancient world, funeral urns were decorated with works of art, sarcophagi were chiselled out of stone, and even pyramids were built to protect the bodies of the dead. The Egyptians embalmed their dead and buried them with objects they had used from day to day, to rest almost as if still alive. Today, when an important person dies, they receive solemn rites in public ceremonies. Soldiers who die in battle receive military honours. If their bodies are lost on the battlefield, no effort is spared to recover them.

'So I ask you, why did the dictatorship refuse to return our bodies to our families? Or, in the words of Saint Paul, why denigrate someone who has already died? The answer, as Paul says, is to conceal the evidence of the crime, ensure that no trace is left. Concealing the body conceals the crime in all its magnitude. This makes it possible to kill thousands without provoking an immediate reaction, given that society, dumbfounded, takes some time to realize what is happening.

'This method inevitably leads to the suppression of the history of these disappearances by suppressing places of collective memory. Memory is like an imaginary tomb. Churches dedicate basilicas to the apostles, communities build shrines to the saints they believe performed miracles, people visit the graves of artists, poets, musicians. Even philosophical materialists like us revere Lenin's statue, at Finland Station in Saint Petersburg, and leave flowers at Marx's grave in London. By paying tribute to those who were great, we go beyond ourselves, we feel reinvigorated. But the method of disappearance precludes all of that. Soon nothing will remain of us. It's a modern version of *damnatio memoriae*, a terrible Roman law which ordered the destruction of any trace of those whom the state considered a traitor, any image or reminder. The method of disappearance means that our lives are erased; it's as if we had never existed.

'The question is, how does this method re-emerge 2,000 years after the Romans? Who brought it back? It reappeared in Hitler's Night and Fog Decree of December 1941, which ordered the liquidation of members of the resistance in Nazi-occupied Europe. To kill them and leave no trace. Cynically taking inspiration from a poem by Goethe, the decree targeted those whose execution would make them martyrs, or whose death sentence couldn't be guaranteed in a formal trial. It ordered them to be transported to Germany, where they would "vanish without a trace into the night and fog." Later, in the Algerian War, the French generals adopted the method with an even more sinister aim: to silently eliminate thousands of rebels at one fell swoop. French officers then taught the method to Argentine generals, and these to their Brazilian and Chilean counterparts.'

So spoke Rodriguez. A silence followed. Then a murmuring, increasing gradually in volume. I thought of my mother, replacing the grains of rice on the altar to Buddha every morning, so that the spirits of her parents could remain in peace on the other side. And I wondered whether she had placed my portrait next to those of my grandparents, or whether the lack of a burial made it impossible.

David took Rodriguez's place in the pulpit and proposed that the session be closed. But nobody moved. Nobody wanted the night to end there. One minute went by, then another. At the back of the nave, a woman of around thirty stood up and walked to the front, where, without introducing herself, she asked if she could read a poem. She was tall and strong, with striking angular features, blonde hair, blue eyes, and a straight nose. Her voice was calm, rhythmic. Rodriguez whispered to me that she and her husband were the last from our organization to be disappeared, both cremated in the furnace of the sugar mill in Campos dos Goytacazes.

'The poem is called *The Disappeared*,' she said. 'It's by Affonso Romano de Sant'Anna, and it's about us. It's a long poem, so I'm just going to recite my favourite part.

> *At that time, all of a sudden,*
> *people began to disappear,*
> *strangely. People disappeared.*
> *They disappeared a lot back then.*
>
> *One might go to gather flowers*
> *and vanish.*
> *One could be eclipsed between one address*
> *and another, in a departing taxi.*
> *Guilty or not, one might disappear*
> *on the way home from the office,*
> *or from an orgy.*
> *A drinker would disappear*
> *between one glass of brandy and a signal to*
> *the barman for another.*
> *A father evaporated on the way*
> *to meet his daughter, who had vanished too.*
> *Mothers clutching at children and bags of shopping,*
> *pregnant women busy with their knitting,*
> *groups of students*
> *disappeared.*
> *Lovers disappeared in mid-kiss*
> *as did surgeons in theatre.*

Just as they turned on their lathe
for the day, mechanics faded.
People disappeared.
People disappeared a lot back then.

People disappeared in plain sight
and it wasn't short-sightedness.
People even disappeared at first sight.
It was enough for someone to see
the disappeared,
and the disappeared would disappear.
The most conspicuous disappeared
and the most hidden too.
Even deputies and presidents vanished.
Priests went floating into the beyond,
insubstantial, to see how fishermen departed.

People disappeared. People disappeared
a lot back then.
Actors on stage
between one gesture and the next,
and those in the audience, while laughing.
No, it wasn't easy to be a poet back then.
Because the poets, more than anyone
— disappeared.'

She bowed forward slightly, marking the end of the reading, and returned to the far end of the nave.

Someone piped up from the back with a question. 'Comrade Rodriguez, didn't disappearance inspire any myths?'

'It inspired Sebastianism in Portugal,' replied Rodriguez, 'at the end of the 1500s. Sebastianism was the belief in the return of King Sebastião, who had disappeared in the battle of Alcácer Quibir, and in the grandeur of the Portuguese Empire, which was in decline. In antiquity, the most relevant myth is that of King Set, from Egyptian mythology. Set envied his brother Osiris, who was king of another part of Egypt, and he dismembered his body, scattering the pieces, just as they did to some of those here. Isis, Osiris' wife, manages to gather the pieces and put him together, and he comes back to life. But it's more a myth of resurrection than it is of disappearance.'

Several hands went up, people began talking over one another.

David took control of the meeting again, warning that it was already past midnight. He gave Rubens the floor.

Rubens walked up to the pulpit with measured strides. He was older than most of those present; he had been around forty when the police brought him in on some minor pretext and disappeared him. People say he was buried and exhumed three times, before finally being thrown into the sea.

'My countrymen and women, we mustn't allow a repeat of the atrocities which so afflicted my generation. We must fight. I address in particular the workers and students who have been so harmed by neoliberal fascism. My daughter was just fifteen when she was arrested. They put a hood over her head and terrorized her for three days and three nights; she took years to accept that I was dead. My wife spent eleven days in jail; she took twenty-five years to accept I was never coming back. Twenty-five years! That shows you the cruelty of the method of disappearance. This cruelty had a *raison d'être*, it was the means of exterminating entire political movements: the socialists in Chile, the Peronists in Argentina, the patriots in Brazil. Nearly 10,000 murdered in Chile, of whom more than 3,000 were disappeared. In Argentina there were 9,000 disappeared, and they're just the ones we have names for. There were hundreds, maybe thousands, of whom not even a name remains. Those dictators decided who could live and who should die. I would like to remind comrade Rodriguez of another principle of Roman law, that of *Homo Sacer* – people whose lives anyone could take without fear of punishment, without even having to explain themselves. They were disposable people, and we were the disposable people of Brazil. Today, faced with a fascism which takes advantage of lies, violence, and coercion, we know how much we are needed. Disappearance never again! Fascism never again!'

So spoke Rubens, the former congressman.

I noticed that the word 'disposable' had caused a stir. In our time, this concept hadn't existed. But if it were true, I thought, then our deaths had been decided a long time before we were killed. It wasn't because we took up arms, it wasn't because of anything we did or didn't do, it was because of who we were. And before us, it was the Indigenous peoples, and after us, the people living in favelas.

A murmuring grew louder and louder, filling the nave. David asked for silence and called on Pedro Tim.

'Comrades, before I was disappeared, I lost two brothers who drowned and a son who was taken ill when he was still very small. But we got through these losses, with the support of friends and relatives. By mourning, we purged our pain, transforming loss into memory, and this way the family came together. But in disappearance this is all subverted. The murdering state imposes a different liturgy of death, a macabre liturgy which keeps us suspended for an eternity between pain and hope. It traps us in the fruitless search for a body which has been deliberately withheld, and finally, it plunges us into perpetual melancholy. For more than forty years, our families have suffered the melancholy of the absent body. Thank you.'

David called on the next person on the list, Joca.

A man of around thirty stood up and walked over to the pulpit. He had a narrow face, framed by a head of thick black hair. As he passed me, I noticed his tense expression. On my list I had the following notes: a worker, born in Italy, the only foreigner who fought in the Araguaia campaign. He refused to surrender after being ambushed by an army patrol and was shot. He was one of the last to die. He spoke with an accent:

'For years on end, my mother knocked on every door, begging for the right to give me a proper burial. She never gave up hope. But they always told her, Dona Elena, we don't have any records. Fifty years have gone by, and they're still concealing me. So even if identification of our remains is becoming increasingly unlikely, I think it should be our principal objective. That's no comfort to my mother, who died embittered, as if she had failed in some way, but it will be for other families and for people in general. I don't see this new fascism as a huge issue, it's a calamity which one day will pass. But I think about the people of Brazil, the good ones at least, a nation which cannot be at peace knowing that so many of its children remain unburied. Thank you.'

Then it was the turn of Tuti, a big lad, tall and with strong features. He had wounds all over his body and his nose had been disfigured.

'My mother also moved heaven and earth to recover my body. In the end she became such a nuisance that they killed her too, faking a car accident. Let's be realistic, most of the officials who know where we were dumped are no longer alive. Too much time has been lost, precious years; the search should have begun as soon as the dictatorship fell, in the first days, the first hours, but there was so much to do, the struggle for amnesty, the new constitution, reparations. I'm not criticizing our comrades; we were all victims in one way or another. Our bodies will never be found, but our spirits live on as a projection of our values, our personal and family relationships, and our political and historical consciousness. There needs to be a permanent venue where they can meet. I propose we fight for the creation of a centre of research, memory, and documentation about us; this will also be our meeting place. I know it won't be easy, but I think this should be our goal. Thank you.'

David called Jonas. He got to his feet with difficulty from the pews in the front row. He was bald, and a scar on his head was visible; a bone protruded through the skin of his right forearm. He tried to stand tall, puffing his chest out exaggeratedly. Eyes flashing, he addressed the audience.

'Comrades, it was the impunity of the death squads which paved the way for the terrorist state, and it was the impunity of the terrorist state which paved the way for the outbreak of fascism. I know that many years have gone by, but it's never too late for society to face up to the atrocities of the dictatorship. This is the only way we will create a widespread repudiation of terrorism, whether that of the state, or of fascist gangs.'

He let a few seconds go by and then shouted, 'Viva Marighella!'

From the back of the cathedral, someone shouted, 'Viva!'

'Viva!' echoed a few isolated voices, though I was struck by how few joined in.

An uncomfortable silence descended, which was only broken when David called the next person on the list, Nira. A woman of around thirty with striking good looks ascended the pulpit. She looked like a film star.

'Comrades, I won't keep you long. I was one of six siblings; we were very close. My brothers and sisters went months and months without asking anyone about my whereabouts, scared that if I was alive and they were to say anything they would blow my cover. But I was dead. I had been dead since the first day. That's how perverse the method of disappearance is. Thank you.'

David called the next on the list, Maranhão. A man of around fifty got up. He had thinning hair, an oval face and an intense gaze which swept the nave as if gauging the atmosphere. He had been a congressman and one of the most senior leaders of the party. He chose his words carefully, speaking with a strong northeastern accent.

'Comrades, I think it was a mistake to accept an amnesty law which pardoned crimes against humanity. Some things are negotiable; others are not. A crime against humanity is not negotiable. The law was poorly conceived. It created an equivalence between the guilty and the innocent, as if it were possible for torturers and their victims to share the same project of democratic transition. That's what led to the outbreak of fascism. And not only was the National Truth Commission created too late and without any power to punish, it didn't even set out to find our remains. This was wrong. I propose we demand a revision of the Amnesty Law, to ensure that those accused of crimes against humanity are put on trial. It's not enough just to punish the thugs of today. The fascist threat will only recede once we have settled scores with the past.'

And so they spoke, one after another, making proposals and offering glimpses into family dramas. Few of the younger ones spoke. One young woman revealed that her disappearance had divided her family, as her father was a supporter of the dictatorship and didn't change his stance even after she was disappeared. In the end, the family fell apart.

One elderly man, with a wrinkled face and soft eyes, said something which made an impression on me: 'I was about to turn sixty when they took me away, and I had five daughters, as well as all my siblings, cousins, uncles and godparents. When a misfortune has many relatives, it is even greater.'

I found out from David that he was called Nestor, he played the clarinet and produced the party newspaper for the peasant movement. Nestor was surprised by the scarce numbers of peasants in the congress. He said that many of them had been disappeared, far more than accounted for by the official list. He proposed that searches be organized to reveal their identities. By the time Nestor finished, a weak light was beginning to filter through the stained-glass windows of the cathedral. That was when David closed the opening session of the First National Meeting of the Disappeared.

9.

It was the second night of the congress. David, Fátima, and I waited at the entrance to the cathedral to welcome the new arrivals. A small, close-knit group appeared at the top of the stairs, with one determined-looking type at the front who seemed to be the leader.

'That's Pedro Carretel,' said Fátima, 'one of the local settlers who joined the guerrilla campaign.'

When they arrived they were all frowning, but their expressions transformed when they saw Fátima, and they exchanged hugs and greetings. After a short conversation, they entered the cathedral. Soon afterwards, several young men unknown to us arrived, one after the other, as if they had all come from different places.

We waited there for another five minutes and were just about to go in when some latecomers turned up. They had travelled far to be there. I recognized Luiz Renato, who had been disappeared in Bolivia, but there were two I didn't know, who David introduced as Túlio and Luiz Carlos, both disappeared in Chile under Pinochet. David said that Túlio had been arrested with his wife; they let her go, but shot him. As for Luiz Carlos, it was said he had been machine-gunned by seventy soldiers, when he was just twenty-five.

We entered. In the immensity of the central nave there was a constant hum of conversation. They sounded more enthusiastic, more relaxed, than during the opening session. The dim light was soothing; the tension of the first night seemed to have evaporated. There were now 182 of us, though there was still no sign of Amarildo. I wondered if he would ever show up. David opened the session and greeted the new arrivals. Warning that the list of speakers was long, he called on Heleny to begin.

A woman of around thirty walked down the aisle and climbed up to the pulpit. She had long dark hair and a graceful, oval face. She wore a severe expression. I had met her before, though we had been members of different organizations. She didn't mince her words.

'Comrades, many of you know me from Tiradentes Prison; after my release, I was kidnapped and then disappeared. I was a philosophy graduate; I was into theatre and art and politics. Like Rodriguez, I was fascinated by mythology. I agree with David, in that we should look to the future; the defeat has been a learning experience. Yes, we should resume the struggle, but on a different level this time. We must create narratives of hope and redemption, engaged with today's world, with the new, and not only through political action, but through art, culture, theatre, cinema, social media, to fight against racism and the oppression of women and of sexual diversity. Thank you.'

David called on Osvaldão, who was next on the list. A ripple of anticipation went through the crowd; Osvaldão, the legendary hero of the Araguaia campaign, was about to speak. The silence was total.

'Comrades, what I'm about to say will explain the absence of some of those who fought in Araguaia. I'm going to tell you what I know, what I saw with my own eyes, without hiding anything. This is no fairytale. On our side there was desertion and betrayal; on the army's side there were abuses and atrocities. But we must separate what is false from what is true. I was the pioneer, the first to arrive in Bico do Papagaio in 1966. I worked as a fisherman, hunter, boatman, miner; I did a bit of everything. I made friends, I started a family. And all the while I was doing the reconnaissance, drawing the maps. The local people were poor, long-suffering.

'When our comrades began to arrive, it was me who told them where to settle, where to buy land, where to open a business. One part of our group settled in Chega Com Jeito, near the land belonging to Zé do Onça; some others went to Palestina, close to the Serra das Andorinhas; and another group bought a farm in São Geraldo, in the Caianos region. Juca set up a hospital in Amaro. Dina opened a pharmacy; she gave injections free of charge and worked as a midwife. Chica taught the local kids to read and write.

'In the mornings we would hunt, fish, gather nuts, and help out in the community. In the afternoons we would go out into the forest and dig holes in different places where we would hide our ammunition, salt, provisions, and medical supplies; these were to keep us going once the fighting began. All the political preparation, the reading and training, took place after dark, all of it in total secrecy. It gets dark early in the forest. It was a peaceful time, but it was tough as well, and there were setbacks.

'Some lost their nerve and left. It's not easy living in such an isolated place, three miles from your closest neighbour, sleeping in hammocks. Lots of rain, mosquitoes, insects that wouldn't give us any peace. Nilo begged us to let him go. We gave in, took him to the highway, even gave him some cash, then later we found out that he had been arrested on the spot and beaten senseless. Pedro Albuquerque and his wife Ana took advantage when we were distracted and ran away. Carlos feigned an illness and took off. Lena even left her husband to turn herself in. These incidents should have served as warnings, but we didn't let them affect us, we just stuck to our routine. That was our first mistake.

'Meanwhile, the leaders wrote. They were the ideologues, the men of letters. Cid wrote a history book to mark fifty years of the party. Joaquim wrote reports he shared with the other party bosses. Old Mário wrote a diary. He was almost blind when he was killed. People said it was river blindness, brought on by the bite of the blackfly, but it was just old age.

'Six years went by like this, just preparing. Six years in the forest is an age! They arrived as boys and girls, but toughened up, became men and women. Not six weeks, nor six months, but six years, and without the locals knowing a thing. And if it had been ten years, it would've been the same. How were we supposed to win hearts and minds, pretending to be something we weren't? Never mind organize an uprising. And yet, at the same time, we were more and more impatient for battle. When the first troops arrived, we even celebrated.

'It was a joyful moment: finally, the popular war which we had so longed for was about to begin. I celebrated too. But we were deluded! We got off to a bad start, a horrible start, years of preparation and they caught us off guard. We fled into the forest leaving a lot of our equipment behind, the only radio, our medical supplies. After the attack, we split into three groups, isolated from one another. Then the supplies began to run out. The hunger was agonizing. But the worst was the lack of salt and medicines. As I said, this is no fairytale. We had been betrayed. Old Mário thought that it was Nilo, but today we know it was Pedro Albuquerque, and a long way from Araguaia. He had been picked up while renewing some official documents in Fortaleza and tortured.

'At first the locals were on our side, but that didn't last for long, one of them denounced Maria and she was shot. From that moment everything changed, we started to see the locals as the enemy, the order was to make contact with them only when strictly necessary and only when we were certain there were no soldiers or informants around. When Neuza went into labour Juca was called, and Gil and Flávio went with him. Someone warned the army and they sent a patrol. All three of them were shot. Who tipped off the military? I still don't know. When Zeca Fogoió asked one of the locals for a meal, the wife put rat poison in the food and sent out her boy to get the army. Many died in ambushes, betrayed by the locals. Joaquim and Old Mário glorified them as the masses; for us they were just peasants.

'Now I come to the worst part of my story. The army left for almost a year. That was when we should have organized a withdrawal, but the view of the commanders was that if they returned, even in greater numbers, we would be ready for them and the battle would become the great protracted people's war. It was Joaquim who was in charge; it would have been his decision to withdraw, but he never gave the order. This was another mistake.

'In the second campaign, not wanting to get bogged down in the forest, the army threatened and tortured the locals for information. They took their flour, their rice, all their provisions. They torched their houses. They hung people upside down, they beat them. One peasant, Clóvis, spent eight days on the *pau de arara*. Another one, Hermógenes, was thrown in a hole they called Vietnam. These people have been forgotten, because they were poor, but a lot of them got hurt, traumatized for the rest of their lives. Carretel, who is here, can back me up on this. A few of the older ones still talk about it today, I hear them in the bars in the evenings, talking in whispers. In Bom Jesus do Araguaia they ran everybody out of town and locked up all the men; the women and girls all ran away, some of them were forced into prostitution. There are people who were driven mad.

'And all the while we had no contact with the party leaders, no logistical support, no nothing. We're talking about a party with fifty years' experience of working in clandestinity, and we didn't even have an emergency contact. We tried to survive by hunting. Things got even worse. When the army came back, they were under orders not to leave anyone alive. Those who were captured were taken to a farm called Fazenda Consolação, where they were executed. Or the army took them out into the forest, telling them they were doing reconnaissance, and then shot them in the back. Even those already in custody were killed. And two years after it was all over they were still killing anyone who knew anything about it. They would organize parties, lay on an accordionist, *cachaça*, then make a note of anyone who shot their mouth off and later that person would be disappeared. Even today, the people of Araguaia are scared of talking about it. This was clear in the hearings of the National Truth Commission in Marabá, I went to them all.

'In October of 1973 they ambushed Alfredo, Nunes, Zé Carlos, and Zebão skinning a pig. They machine-gunned the four of them and left their bodies in the forest. On 26th November they decapitated Ari, and then the next week they did the same to Chicão. They paid 1,000 cruzeiros per head, which was enough to buy a piece of land. The heads were taken to the commanding officer and then transported to Belém in a cool box with ice. As far as I know, there were four who were decapitated: Ari, Jaime, Chicão, and Mundico. Ari was a physics student. He was twenty-five when the woodsman Iomar shot him in the chest. They say he was still moving when Iomar took a blunt machete to his neck. Just imagine, cutting off the head of someone still alive. We buried the body without the head, at the foot of a *jatobá* tree. I oversaw the burial and made sure he was given all the appropriate honours. In the case of Mundico, I only know what I've been told, though I think it's true. They came looking for his head after he had been killed; they dug him up and decapitated the body, just like the government troops used to do with the bandits in the Northeast. It was savage.

'Then there was the Christmas Massacre, when on Christmas Day they ambushed fifteen of our comrades and killed four of them, including Old Mário and Pedro Gil, both members of the Military Command. By that point it was basically all over. We had no leadership and most of those who managed to escape into the forest were soon caught. Two days later we regrouped. Joaquim and I said that anyone who wanted to leave was free to go. This was tacit recognition that the campaign was finished. But out of twenty-five of us, not one raised their hand. How do you explain that? Were we afraid of being labelled as cowards? I don't know, all I know is that either Joaquim or I should have ordered a withdrawal, as he was a commander and I was a veteran, the most experienced. It shouldn't have been a question of personal choice or a matter of bravery, but a political decision. Joaquim and Cid have received burial and are no longer among us, but Old Mário is present and can share his thoughts. I'm not here to judge anyone, nor criticize. But I am sorry for my part in this mistake.

'After that we split into groups of five. The hunger was unbearable, so much so that some of us asked the locals for food, knowing full well it would mean our capture and execution. By that point they were all collaborating with the military, whether out of fear or conviction. The army had us all on a list. We were hunted down like animals, one by one. Simão couldn't take it anymore and asked for help from one of the riverside people, thinking they'd take pity on him. Not a chance – he and Raul were taken up to Brejo Grande and shot. He can tell you what happened. Raul was picked up half-starved and sick. He had been a cheerful kid, a biochemistry and pharmacy student, a Flamengo supporter. A local found his body after the animals had got to it. Lia got lost amongst some rocks and was found almost starving. And so many others, Antônio Alfaiate, Beto, Valdir, Áurea. Poor Áurea, she was a mess by the time she was found by some woodsmen. They discovered Jaime in a shack, his leg all consumed by leishmaniasis.

'Now do you understand why some of them haven't come to the congress? One of the last to die was Dina. She died looking her killers in the eye. Forty-one were shot, without mercy. There was no need; they had already surrendered, they were unarmed. It was a war crime. The army still claims Tuca and another six struck deals and live under new identities, but it's a slander. By February 1974 there was nothing left of the campaign, just a handful of fighters still lost in the forest, so what intelligence could they possibly have given the army?

'At first the military just denied flat out that there had ever been a guerrilla campaign; they'd committed too many atrocities to admit it. All the while they were covering their tracks, there were three expeditions just to dig up the bodies and cremate them. Now, as there's no way of denying it, they distort history. What I've heard directly from comrades and in the hearings of the National Truth Commission in Marabá contradicts any suggestion that deals were made. Piauí endured three months of torture, without giving up anything, so they shot him. His torturer, Chico Dólar, showed the documents concerning the executions of Piauí, Ari Armeiro, Duda, Rosinha, and Josias. Another official, Vanu, witnessed the executions of Piauí and Duda. The only one who may have been spared was Edinho, not because he made a deal – by the time they picked him up there was nothing left to say – but because he was from a military family. It's true that during all this time I've never once encountered him, but even so I doubt he survived, because there are navy and army records of his death and Vanu said that he witnessed his execution.

'All of these people are missed today. They would be leaders. Joaquim managed to escape with help from Zezinho but ended up dead in the Lapa Massacre, in São Paulo. As for Cid, he wasn't even there when the army first attacked, he had gone to an event to celebrate the party's fiftieth anniversary. Ironic, don't you think? He was uncompromising on the issue of the popular war, but ended up living to ninety and died peacefully in his own bed.

'Now, I ask you: what can we take from all of this? I still don't know what to make of it. We held out for nearly three years. There were three incursions by the army, each one bigger than the one before. They had to send more than 1,000 soldiers to deal with just a handful of us. As I've said, it's a sad story. It's about the deaths of young people who had their whole lives ahead of them, who could've become political leaders, or famous artists. I keep going over it in my mind. José Carlos had only just turned twenty when he was sent to the Chinese Military Academy. Duda dropped out of a medical degree at twenty to join the guerrillas. Two kids. Áurea was just nineteen when she went to Araguaia. Most of them were yet to turn thirty. That's what still feels bitter, the blow that still hurts today.'

Osvaldão descended from the pulpit. There was no reaction, not a single sound. The silence was absolute. We weren't expecting any kind of triumphalist narrative, but the rawness of his testimony was devastating. Some minutes went by. Then an old man got to his feet at the back of the nave and took two steps forward, leaning on a younger man for support. There was murmuring: 'It's Old Mário, Old Mário's going to speak.' His appearance was striking: he had a broad face, a high forehead and a prominent, aquiline nose. The younger man helping him was his son Zé Carlos. From Old Mário's cautious steps it was clear that he was blind. David stepped down from the pulpit and welcomed the old man with solemnity.

'Comrades! This congress is a great achievement. They tried to wipe us off the face of the Earth, but here we are, for a new day of struggle. Comrade Osvaldão has described the horrors of the final moments of some of our comrades who are not present. I call on them to attend. They have nothing to be ashamed of. The Araguaia campaign was a great event, a glorious chapter of our history, and the ideas behind it are eternal. I know that we have many critics, but if mistakes were made then they were tactical, not strategic.

'For my part, since our party's fifth congress I have defended the position that it is impossible to achieve social justice and national sovereignty without recourse to the armed struggle, given the nature of the dominant powers in our country. It is a fallacy to say that social democracy will come as a natural consequence of capitalist development; our capitalism has retained in its very essence the same relations of production as slavery. The times have changed, the names have changed, but this essence remains the same. The proof of this lies in the fascist assault on the Three Branches of Government. I recognize that today an armed response is unthinkable, but words alone aren't enough. We must organize, raise awareness, mobilize, so that popular forces may overcome the fascist militias by occupying our streets and squares. This congress is an important step forward in this direction. Our belief in the triumph of socialism remains unshakeable.'

The old man descended from the pulpit and went slowly back to his seat, leaning on his son for support. So many lives wasted, and not a trace of remorse, I thought.

David let a few seconds pass and then called on Pedro Carretel to speak.

'Comrades, I never had the chance to study. Everything I know I learnt at the school of hard knocks, and I joined the comrades from São Paulo because I understood that the fight was a just one. What I ask you is this: if the cause was just, why was God so cruel towards our families? My wife Isaura was so traumatized by what happened she lost her mind. It's not human, it's not Christian, nor anything else. I think they might have talked about this yesterday, but I missed it. If someone can fill me in, I'd be grateful.'

Fátima was next on the list. She headed to the pulpit, limping, though her posture was erect. Her speech was brief and to the point.

'Comrades, our memories are not ours alone. They belong to the people and they mustn't be lost, they have ethical and political value. I support Tuti's proposal to fight for the creation of a centre of documentation. I also propose that we immediately begin collecting testimony from each and every one of us about how we were disappeared. This will also help to put an end, once and for all, to the slander spread by the army. Thank you.'

David called Simão, who walked slowly towards the pulpit.

'Comrades, I dropped everything to join the guerrillas. A loving family, an attentive godfather, a job, studies … I left it all behind. When I left, I had only just turned twenty. By the time I surrendered, I felt like an old man. As soon as I arrived in Araguaia I regretted my decision. I had been a happy person, but there, I was overcome with a great sadness, an infinite sadness. After a while I started to rally, to recover my spirits, there were times when I even rediscovered my belief in the struggle. But I should've turned back the very same day I arrived. What did we know about the protracted people's war? Nothing! What did we know about the people of Araguaia? Nothing! Absolutely nothing. How could we, at such a young age? Those who sent us to Araguaia should have known, but not us.

And here we are today, spectres of ourselves, and we can see that many of those same people we wanted to liberate prefer fascism. I think the whole thing was crazy. While the feeling of regret has now passed, the remorse for the pain I caused my parents has never left me. I'd like to apologize to my godfather and to my family.'

Simão descended slowly from the pulpit and returned to his place. David let some time go by, for people to absorb his testimony and perhaps to respond. But no hand went up. The silence was heavy. David called on João Marinheiro.

A lad of around twenty whom I vaguely recognized ascended the pulpit. He was one of those betrayed by Cabo Anselmo. He began calmly, but as he went on, he raised his voice, filled with bitterness.

'Comrades, I'm sorry for what I'm about to say, but I only came to this congress so I could say it. The Brazilian people don't deserve our sacrifice. We fought and died in vain. The capitalists are what they are. But what is shocking is just how many ignoramuses, imbeciles, and lowlifes there are amongst the population. There's no point in trying to raise the awareness of an idiot or a lowlife. I am mortified that I gave my life for these people.'

João Marinheiro's speech provoked some commotion; many people wanted to respond. Unfazed, David followed the order on the list and called on Onofre, who had spoken the previous night.

'Comrades, I'm from a military background. I think it was a mistake to have accepted the Amnesty Law. Everywhere else, the murderers and torturers in the military were put on trial and punished, but not in Brazil. For the next congress, I propose we invite the Chilean and Argentine disappeared. Our struggle is the same, and we need to learn from them. Of course we can't invite them all, that would be impractical, but we could ask each country to send a delegation. Thank you.'

David called on Ivanildo to speak. An older gentleman, with a large forehead and a narrow jaw, headed to the pulpit. I recognized him from my student days, he had been secretary to Governor Miguel Arraes. I knew his real name wasn't Ivanildo. His speech was impassioned.

'I don't share João Marinheiro's disillusionment. I know the Brazilian people will make amends for their mistakes. But don't delude yourselves into thinking that the calamity the country has undergone is over. I tell you this with conviction: the pact between the evangelical masses, the petite bourgeoisie, and the rapacious capitalists isn't a temporary thing, it's here to stay. This is a sinister pact which has brought out the very worst things concealed in the darkest depths of the human soul, dishonesty, inhumanity, indifference, and cynicism. It's an alliance of evil, which will only generate more destitution and sadness. They tried once to bring down the Republic and they will try again. We have a long period of darkness ahead of us. The fascist death drive has no limit, so I predict some bleak times, worse even than the Years of Lead of our youth.'

It sounded like a bad omen. Most of those present were silent, though some seemed displeased, gesticulating or shaking their heads. João Marinheiro asked for the floor and spoke in a thunderous tone from his place in the nave.

'We've already sacrificed ourselves to fix the country and look where we ended up. It's down to the young, because it's another world now, it's not our world anymore.'

David called Beto, the last on the list. A hush descended and I felt the tension increase. At the back, a shape straightened up and walked towards the pulpit, with slow footsteps. Osvaldão whispered to me: they had been three siblings, all murdered in Araguaia.

'I'm Beto. I don't know if my words will reach my parents, but I'm speaking to ask for their forgiveness. I was the oldest child; it was my duty to protect my brother and sister, and I failed. Maria fell in the first days, though at that time we still couldn't foresee the defeat, or that we would all end up getting killed. Jaime and I could still be alive, we were arrogant, we had no right to inflict on our parents the loss of three children. May our family forgive us. Thank you.'

Beto returned to the depths of the nave.

David gestured towards the stained-glass windows. 'It's getting light,' he said, 'we must close the session, but before we do, I would like to respond to Ivanildo. There's no doubt that these days are even more difficult than those of our youth. These are medieval times; look at the militias, the massacres, the hatred of culture. And it's not only here, look at all the disasters one after another, the great floods, the endless wildfires, the spread of hunger and destitution, and with them, violence. Our grandchildren should be ready for some hard times.'

So spoke David, and on this sombre note he closed the second night of the congress.

10.

I spent the morning thinking about the decapitations. Why bother cutting off the head of someone who is already dead? The only explanation I could think of was to spread fear, but for that to happen the head must be displayed in public, like that of Tiradentes, or the execution carried out on camera, as in the case of the Islamic State. But in Araguaia the decapitations were hidden.

That afternoon, in the square, I asked Rodriguez if any insights could be found in mythology.

'When you cut off a head,' he said, 'in a single gesture you appropriate the life and the mind of the other. The Celts preserved the heads of their most formidable enemies in oil and they wouldn't exchange them for anything.'

'And in modern times? Why did they use the guillotine in the French Revolution when they could have just shot them?'

'The guillotine symbolized the decapitation of the idle classes, not just individuals. It was the nobility and the clergy that were being decapitated, that's why they were guillotined en masse and in public squares.'

'What about in Araguaia? Most of our comrades were dead already.'

'Decapitating someone who is already dead happens a lot in Africa,' said Rodriguez. 'The intention is to debase the human condition of the victim, and it's also a message of terror written using the human body.'

He paused to reflect for a moment, then said, 'They might have taken their heads to identify them, given there was confusion between names and codenames. Whatever the reason, it's grotesque, but it's part of the culture of the Brazilian Army. They've always cut throats, and that's almost tantamount to decapitation.'

'They've always cut throats? Since when?'

'It dates back to the Paraguayan War, which was the war that really established the army. It was called the "red cravat". The Duke of Caxias used to brag about not taking prisoners, and cutting throats was the cheapest method, it meant they saved on bullets. The practice persisted during the period of the Republic – the man responsible for the Canudos Massacre, Colonel Antônio Moreira César, was known as the "head-cutter".'

'Where did you get all this from?' I asked.

'From books. It's all there, I'm not making anything up. In Canudos they cut the throats of poor farmers, certain of impunity, and this certainty became ingrained, part of the culture. By the way, did you know the Duke of Caxias wasn't really called Caxias, and he wasn't even a noble?'

'I didn't.'

'He was a colonel called Luis Alves de Lima e Silva,' Rodriguez explained. 'He was awarded the title of Baron of Caxias for having put down an uprising of slaves and subsistence farmers who had occupied the town of Caxias in Maranhão. Twelve thousand died in that massacre alone.'

I thought about the bodies of Jorge and Osvaldão suspended from helicopters for all the locals to see, and I said, 'The government troops used to display the heads of the bandits they killed in the Northeast, to dispel the myth of invincibility which surrounded the outlaw Lampião. Do you think that was why they displayed the body of Osvaldão in Araguaia?'

'Maybe,' said Rodriguez, 'that's what they did to Zumbi dos Palmares. They put his head on a pike in Recife to put an end to the belief that he was immortal. But it was also just the standard punishment used by the Portuguese Crown for anyone who rebelled. And there's another explanation. Did you know that in medieval England they cut off the heads of those defeated in battle? It was to prevent their ghosts from returning to haunt the living and demanding justice, an event they called the Apocalypse of the Spectres. It terrified them. So perhaps, on some level, the military were scared of the resurrection of the guerrillas.'

'Why apocalypse?' I asked.

Rodriguez launched straight into another lesson, this time from the Bible.

'The apocalypse is the myth of the end of the world. At the same time, it's salvationist – it predicts the rise of a new order, following the destruction of the world through a series of catastrophes. This idea was very widespread in the Middle Ages. The most famous version is from the last book of the New Testament, the Book of Revelation, attributed to John the Apostle. His version is certainly one of the most extraordinary and shocking. The narrator threatens the idolaters, adulterers, and all who sin against the Christian commandments with horrific punishments. Then he relates dreams and visions of seven terrible plagues, worse than the flood and the plagues of Egypt, and then finally a mass extinction led by the Four Horsemen of the Apocalypse, terrifying characters who spread hunger, war, death, and disease.'

'It sounds like a horror movie,' I said.

'It's worse than a horror movie. There's a phrase in the Book of Revelation which says: "And in those days shall men seek death and shall not find it; and shall desire to die and death shall flee from them."'

'Does the Bible say when all this is supposed to happen?'

'Yes, it talks about 1,000 years until the advent of the new order, or a new Jerusalem, as some verses say. That's why messianic or salvationist movements, like those led by Antônio Conselheiro in the Canudos uprising or the monk José Maria in the Contestado War, are also called millenarian.'

'Two thousand years have gone by since John's time, and there's been no apocalypse,' I said.

'Some say it has already happened, that the apocalypse was the First World War or the Spanish Flu. But the world didn't end. Then we had the Second World War, the Holocaust, Hiroshima, and the world didn't end; then Chernobyl, and the world didn't end; then the Covid pandemic, and the world didn't end.'

'With the way things seem to be going at the moment, another apocalypse can't be far away,' I said.

'That's right,' Rodriguez said. He fell quiet for a moment, then said, 'And the world won't end.'

11.

It was getting late, just two hours until the congress resumed. But Simão's melancholy speech the previous night had given me pause for thought.

'Why is it,' I asked Rodriguez, 'that some of the youngsters, who weren't even in clandestinity, who had no need to hide, like Simão, dropped everything, their studies, their jobs, to go and live in the forest?'

'Because they were ordered to do so by the party. You heard what Osvaldão said, the party's word was sacred.'

'No-one was forcing them,' I said, 'they could have refused.'

'That would have meant abandoning a whole way of life. Besides, the order was recognition of the militant's worth, a show of trust. Who could refuse?'

'Or maybe they went out of a sense of adventure?'

'That too,' admitted Rodriguez. 'All of a sudden some kid of eighteen finds himself on a plane to China on a secret mission. That taste of adventure removes your ability to think. But it goes beyond that. We were all writing slogans on walls when we were as young as fourteen. Me, you, all of us, it was through our political militancy that we became who we are, and so the decision to join the armed struggle was something that came naturally.'

'And how do you assess the role of the leaders? They had been through so much, they should have known that the conditions weren't right. It was the time of the Economic Miracle!'

'I think for Cid it became an obsession. Have you read his book? It's called *To Fight is My Word*.'

'Obviously it's about political struggle,' I said, 'not about picking fights with just anyone.'

'Think about it,' said Rodriguez, 'a whole lifetime of defeats, and then you get Fidel's victory in the Sierra Maestra, a handful of guerrillas topple a dictatorship and install socialism in the Americas. That had a profound impact on the party veterans, and the military coup gave them a sense of urgency.'

'It was a scandal,' I said, 'so many lives sacrificed, and Old Mário was still asking for reinforcements, more young people, physically strong and ideologically prepared.'

'And willing to sacrifice themselves,' said Rodriguez, 'he let that phrase slip in the letter he wrote the leaders asking for reinforcements. It reminded me of the myth of the Minotaur, the half-man half-bull monster who devoured successive offerings of young people. Old Mário's labyrinth was the jungle, with its winding paths and streams, where the militants became lost before being devoured by the repression. So many pointless deaths, such a waste.'

'I don't understand. What do you mean by a pointless death? Isn't all death pointless?'

'In the Palmares Quilombo there were thousands of deaths which weren't pointless. Palmares gave rise to Black pride, the whole Black identity of today. I call this a creative death, though it's not my own invention. In mythology sacramental deaths are creative, they give rise to something new, a new god, or a new species of plant.'

'The Araguaia campaign also became a powerful symbol, almost a myth.'

'That's only because people have mythologized it and played up the role of victim, both of which are depoliticizing. What they're trying to do is to justify a conflict which wasn't necessary.'

'What's a necessary conflict for you?'

'In the Palmares Quilombo they had to defend themselves. The same goes for the Jews in the Warsaw Ghetto. They had to act, there was no way out. But the Araguaia campaign wasn't just unnecessary, it was a strategic error, imprudent even.'

'You're saying that with the benefit of hindsight though,' I said. 'They had no way of knowing how it would end. You say it was imprudent, but I think that if we only ever do what's prudent then there can be no revolution.'

'I agree there's no such thing as a prudent revolution. In fact I'd go further: without passion, there's no possibility of political action. But the idea of the protracted people's war was doomed from the beginning. When the armed struggle was approved at the party congress of 1966, it was decided both that it would be a popular war and that it would be clandestine, which is a blatant contradiction. What's more, it was based on false premises, like the existence of a peasant movement in Bico do Papagaio, when really it was just home to migrants fleeing from drought, adventurers, and other rootless, scattered people.'

'I disagree. They may have been migrants, but they were tough, brave, people who had learnt the hard way. Cid recognizes this in his notes.'

'Cid also said in an interview that they were ignorant and backward, most of them illiterate, and confessed he knew little of their mentality and their feelings. But these were the people he was counting on. And that's not all. Pomar went to China to consult the leaders there, and Zhou Enlai himself advised against the campaign.'

'But wasn't it the Chinese who provided the training?'

'It was a programme for militants from many different countries, it wasn't specific to the Araguaia campaign. The fact of the matter is Zhou Enlai thought it wasn't the right time and when Pomar got back, he warned the leaders, he said it was a mass suicide, those were the very words he used, mass suicide, but it was no use, he ended up getting demoted by Cid. Three others who were trained in China also came back critical of the idea; they too were demoted by Cid, among them Tarzan de Castro, one of those who was picked up and photographed by the Americans in Karachi.'

I said that I found it difficult to understand Cid, Joaquim, and Old Mário, the commanders of the campaign.

'Old Mário and Cid could have been the grandfathers of some of those kids,' I said, 'they should have shown more of the wisdom that comes with experience.'

'I also find it hard to understand,' said Rodriguez, 'the only explanation that occurs to me is that they placed a bet against history, the ultimate bet on a revolution that had always eluded them. You heard Old Mário, "my belief in socialism remains unshakeable". Socialist revolution was the *raison d'être* of the party founders, and after decades of making compromises of one kind or another, these old leaders needed to rediscover the meaning of their lives, and they thought they had found it in the epic story of Chinese socialism. But they never understood the concept of the protracted people's war. In a people's war *everyone* is involved, and their day-to-day tasks are secondary to the war effort. Theirs was a war in the name of the people, but it wasn't a war *of* the people. They set themselves up as the vanguard.'

'We also considered ourselves the vanguard of the proletariat.'

'Yes, but we were acting on impulse; they weren't. It was a project they had planned, based on a belief that had become an obsession. Joaquim and Cid thought they were acting on doctrine, but really it was just a belief, almost like a religion.'

'I disagree,' I said, 'you're reducing everything to subjective factors, as if political ideology didn't exist. And you're downplaying the Araguaia campaign, which the army only defeated through the use of terror and the mobilization of more than 10,000 soldiers. Don't you think there's a certain glory in defeat by such a disproportionate force?'

'In theory, yes, but it depends on how the defeat occurs. There was glory in the mass suicide of the rebel Jews in Masada, in Palmares, perhaps in Canudos, but not in Araguaia, where they were hunted down and picked off one by one. And there weren't 10,000 soldiers, that's an exaggeration. I'm not trying to downplay the campaign, but I want to expand our analysis, using concepts we weren't familiar with at the time, like the role of myth and of belief, for example.'

'Do you think that explains the sacrifice of so many young people?'

'Yes I do, it's something typical of religion. All religions demand sacrifices, offerings to the gods. In this religion, the party leaders were the high priests endowed with the power to decide. The young militants were offered as sacrifice and they accepted their fate.'

'No shit! So that's why, when it had all fallen apart, and Osvaldão asked if any of them wanted to leave, nobody wanted to go?'

'Exactly! It was a rite, a collective sacrifice, and to opt out would have been to negate the entire meaning they had given to their lives. And of course, they were scared of going off alone into the forest.'

Stunned, but not entirely convinced, I asked Rodriguez if he had read Old Mário's diary.

'I have,' he said. 'The tone is epic, he was writing for posterity, describing the coming of a new historical era. It's triumphalist, delusional. At the same time as our comrades were falling one by one, he exalts them. At no point does he recognize the impossibility of the project or express any remorse, nor is there any reflection on the imperative to save the lives of people whom we could have done with today. I think he was in a state of ecstasy, the whole purpose of his existence had been fulfilled. He also accurately describes the insects in the forest, the mosquitos, the ticks, it recalls the diary of Che in Bolivia, he complained about the ticks too. This obsession with keeping a diary, even in the most extreme situations, can only be explained by the leaders' conviction they were chronicling the birth of a new era.'

'What else does he talk about?'

'He talks a lot about food, what they ate from one day to the next. It reminded me of Primo Levi's memoirs. While he was imprisoned at Auschwitz people spoke, thought, and dreamt only of food. Cid was just as delusional as Mário; there's a passage where Old Mário describes him jumping up and down like a child at a ceremony in which they sang the Internationale in the middle of the forest.'

'It can't be easy for Old Mário to face the youngsters; I didn't expect him to turn up.'

'Oh I did. He's a man who gave his life for the revolution. He sees himself as a stoic, a martyr. That's significant.'

I wondered if Marighella had also been willing to make the ultimate sacrifice when he joined the armed struggle.

'The difference,' said Rodriguez, 'is that the Araguaia campaign was based on a plan and it had a specific objective, whereas Marighella acted without any theoretical basis.'

'That's not true,' I said, 'what about the *Minimanual of the Urban Guerrilla*?'

'It's just a summary of some notes he wrote when he was forced into hiding. There's no theory behind it at all, just anger, and instructions on how to rob banks.'

'Again, you're downplaying things, reducing it all to mere impulse. Just a summary of some notes … don't you know that Marighella's manual became world famous?'

'Marighella was also responsible for a lot of unnecessary deaths, although he and Lamarca also managed to inspire thousands of people, they created pockets of support throughout the country, and across all social classes. Why? It was less about achieving some great victory – which wouldn't have been possible in any case – and more about encouraging dissent. It was something very spontaneous, almost anarchist in nature, without any central committee, nobody asked for permission to do this or that.

'In contrast, the Araguaia campaign played out in secret, it didn't need to be silenced as the guerrillas themselves had chosen invisibility as their modus operandi and the army was very happy to keep it that way. Besides which, they never took even a single square metre of territory and apart from springing the odd ambush they were always on the run. It was a total disaster. The leaders created this epic revolutionary narrative, a kind of hagiology of the guerrillas, in which they describe some of the losses as heroic deaths. But it was a disaster, a tragedy. The only reason I won't say they died entirely in vain is because their spectres have now returned to haunt the living.'

So spoke Rodriguez. And in the end, I agreed.

12.

And so the last night of the congress had arrived. More of those disappeared in Araguaia were present; they had probably heard Old Mário's summons. Elisa, Tuca, both of them looking very gaunt, with two lads, Piauí and Duda. Borges didn't show, which cleared up the whole sorry business of the plea bargain. He talked for sure, I thought, he's scared to show his face. Nor had Amarildo come. I asked Rodriguez why not.

'The word must not have reached the places where he tends to drift,' he said.

David announced that as it was the final night, it was time to vote on the proposals made so far and on any others which people might want to make. Heleny raised her hand and asked:

'If we're just spirits, what can we actually do? I've been thinking about this since yesterday. I would like someone to explain what we can and can't do.'

Nobody said anything. After almost a minute, Rodriguez asked for the floor and went up to the pulpit. His speech was a long one.

'I'm going to try and answer Heleny's question. Many of you know of my passion for philosophy. I think that to know what we can do, we need to know what we are. The first point to consider is empirical in nature. We are spectres detached from the animal matter we possessed when we were alive. But we're not just skeletons, we possess the characteristics we had during our lives, as well as an ethereal aura which has preserved our appearance at the moment of death, making us identifiable in the spectral universe. We are icons of who we were in life, incorporeal manifestations of our individual personalities, mental attributes, political consciousness, personal stories, and relationships.

'So, what can we do? A great deal. Our potential is immense, as we have attained a mental state which transcends the material. We can cross obstacles insurmountable to the living and travel unimaginable distances. We also have no need to worry about eating, dressing, and all those other everyday concerns, which allows us to attain full spirituality. There can be no doubt about these characteristics of our condition. What I'm afraid of is that for the living we are nothing at all, that we exist for ourselves, but not for others, as if we were just the creation of our own imaginations. That's what Spinoza, that great philosopher of modernity, would say. For Spinoza, the essence of man is in the unity of body and soul. All human activity – physical, emotional, cognitive – ceases when the body dies. There is nothing left, no soul drifting around. In other words, for Spinoza, we don't exist.'

Consternation spread throughout the nave, increasing in volume, to the point where Rodriguez had to pause. He let nearly a minute go by, then raised his hand, asking for silence. Only then did he resume.

'Calm, comrades, calm. There are 205 of us disappeared here, so in some way, we exist. Not only that, but we can see each other, and certainly we will be visible to those who have reason to fear us, just as the ghost of Hamlet's father appears to his son to demand he avenge his murder. No philosopher has ever really analysed the condition of the disappeared, not the Greeks, nor the modern philosophers. I suggest we correct this omission. We don't have to abandon the struggle to find our remains and to create a memorial, nor do we need to give up the fight against the fascists. These are tasks of a practical nature. But if on top of that, we could also create the basis for a phenomenology of political disappearance, this congress would take on extraordinary dimensions.'

There were murmurs of approval. His speech was fascinating. Who would have thought, that defeated, banished from the worlds of both the living and the dead, we would still be capable of contributing to philosophy?

Rodriguez resumed his speech. 'As philosophy requires precise use of language, I suggest we begin by making a distinction between spirit and soul. For the Greeks, the soul is the sensory dimension of our personality, our feelings and passions, whereas the spirit is our mental essence, made up of the values and the intellectual baggage of each individual. That makes us spirit, but not soul. Another way of making the distinction is by looking at the realms they inhabit. The soul inhabits the memory of those who knew us; it has the same finite existence as they do and it fades as they die or lose their memory. The spirit, on the other hand, is our presence in the collective unconscious of the human species.

'What is the collective unconscious? It's a set of concepts which has been present since the origins of humanity, which we all possess. The psychologist Carl Jung believed we are born with these concepts, that they are a cultural characteristic of the species, not merely of one individual or another. The collective unconscious spans generations; individual memories do not. The Jungian collective unconscious is comprised of beliefs and emblematic characters that he called archetypes. Their origin is in the myths created by prehistoric man to explain the mysteries of nature and the causes of illness. This is how we created the concept of the human, via a web of representations that we spun ourselves.

'Jung found representations of the same archetypes in myths and legends of different peoples, both "primitive" and "modern". The most common is the mother, who protects her child against the father; fertilizes the land, providing good harvests; and protects the fish, like Iemanjá, the goddess of the oceans from the Yoruba myths. Another ubiquitous archetype is the brave hero, which expresses itself in thousands of ways, overcoming obstacles, vanquishing evil, redeeming the people, and foreshadowing a glorious future. There are countless examples of these archetypes, which express the hopes and fears of primitive man. The tyrannical father. The wise old sage. The vile traitor. The wanderer. The wicked stepmother, who brews terrible poisons. The martyr, who sacrifices themselves for their people, like Joan of Arc. The saviour, like Christ and Moses. The ogre, a monster who eats people, appears in many myths, legends, and folk tales.

'There are also mythical narratives which, like archetypes, are present in different cultures. The exodus towards the promised land, resistance down to the last man, or the curse that falls upon a people. The meanings of these narratives are collective. Even our very own Marxist dialectic can be seen as a mythical narrative, in which the ogre is the capitalist monster who feeds on the surplus value of the workers.

'But there is a gap which we have to fill. Jung never found an archetype for the disappeared. He couldn't have, as political disappearance as part of the social imaginary is a phenomenon of our time, essentially post-Jung. So far, we have existed in the transient memories of those who knew us and in collective memories, like those of the Mangueira samba school. But when those who knew us die, and if the culture of Mangueira changes, then we will cease to exist. How can we prevent our definitive erasure? How can we prevent the erasure of the atrocities of which we were the victims? By creating our archetype, the archetype of the disappeared. I think that it's in the universe of the archetypes that we should build our phenomenology of the disappeared, thus ensuring our permanence through time.'

Rodriguez paused, as if to gather his thoughts. From the depths of the nave, where the combatants from Araguaia were gathered, someone asked:

'Comrade Rodriguez, if the spirit is our mental essence, free from the troubles of life, might it be the case that some of the comrades from Araguaia haven't come because they haven't managed to free themselves? Can the spirit overcome anything?'

'It's possible the trauma they suffered was such that their spirits have been unable to free themselves. Why? I don't know. It could be the defeat of the myths they worshipped in their lives, the myth of the revolution, of socialism, it might be the shock of the outbreak of fascism. Or it could be the way they died. The Tupi-Guarani people ritually execute prisoners they capture in battle, so their bravery passes over to their captors. It's the same principle amongst samurai – to go down fighting. But that wasn't the case for many of us. Some were driven to surrender by their hunger; others were shot in the back in cowardly fashion as they fled.'

Rodriguez let some time pass, as if waiting for a response, though none was forthcoming. Then he descended from the pulpit. Murmurs echoed through the great central nave. A minute went by, then two, three. A sensation of discomfort descended on those present. Perhaps they felt daunted by the grandiose undertaking Rodriguez had proposed, I thought, or perhaps it was concern for those from Araguaia who were still absent.

13.

The congress was now drawing to a close, though there was still time for it all to go wrong. A murmuring grew in volume, becoming a clamour. David, who was again chairing the meeting, asked for silence, though it took some time for people to quieten down. He suggested we formed working groups to discuss proposals and asked Rodriguez to put together a summary. We were given an hour.

I counted ten groups scattered throughout the nave. Rodriguez and I stayed at a distance, observing. After an hour, Rodriguez went around each group in turn, listening to what they had to say. I helped, trying to consolidate their ideas. Afterwards, we found a quiet corner and with a little prompting, Rodriguez brought together from memory the ideas that we had heard. After another half hour, and a nod from David, who called the meeting to plenary once more, Rodriguez spoke:

'Comrades, I'm not going to lay out the contributions of each group in detail. Suffice to say that they are substantial. Based on what was discussed, I propose the following basis for a phenomenology of the disappeared:

'*First proposal*: our deaths were neglected. We are beings who crossed the frontier of death, but as we were denied the social rite of burial, were unable to complete our crossing to the other side.

'*Second proposal*: though we are invisible to ordinary mortals, we see other spectres and are seen by them in turn, as well as by those who fear us due to the crimes they committed against us.

'*Third proposal*: we have common demands deriving from our fate and our shared sense of ethics, the most urgent being to locate and identify our remains, so we may receive a proper burial.

'*Fourth proposal*: as we have drifted for so long through non-places, witnessing an infinitude of atrocities and clashes between good and evil, we have accumulated exceptional political wisdom and spiritual energy.

'*Fifth proposal*: we are not innocent, naïve victims of occasional abuses of police power, but militants from social movements, driven by emancipatory ideals, and disappeared by a complex state apparatus precisely for being who we are.

'*Sixth proposal*: along with others who have been subject to political disappearance from all over the world, and throughout history, we constitute the figure of a new archetype. That is the political militant kidnapped by agents of the terrorist state, deprived of all contact with the outside world, tortured, murdered, and finally disappeared, to conceal the crime of which they were victim.

'*Seventh and final proposal*: as archetypes, we symbolize the incessant search of human beings for utopia, as well as their physical fragility and vulnerability before the power of the terrorist state to determine who lives and who dies.'

Rodriguez descended from the pulpit. There was an extended silence. It was a beautiful speech; we had all been moved. We then approved motions of a practical nature, for the recovery of our remains, the creation of a memorial to the disappeared, and the revocation of the amnesty for those accused of crimes against humanity. We also approved a motion repudiating fascism.

To ensure we would be properly prepared, we set a date for the second congress for two years hence, rather than the following year. For the first congress, the objective had been the congress itself. For the second, we chose as our central theme the different ways in which the archetype of the disappeared may express itself, particularly in the most rural and remote pockets of the country.

It was agreed that the congress would take place in the cathedral after the last mass, every even year on 1st May. There was no longer any need to invite anyone. I realized that we were creating our own calendar, with 1st May being our first important date. A committee to organize the second congress was also elected, without me or Rodriguez this time. To our surprise, three out of the five on the committee were young guerrillas from the Araguaia campaign: Chica, Mariadina, and Juca.

14.

That was when something extraordinary happened. We were just starting to disperse, when two men entered the nave: one, a gigantic Black man brandishing an enormous trident; the other, a white man, also tall, bearded, and with flowing blond hair. The Black man was wearing just a loincloth, with a necklace of coloured stones. His expression was determined, his brow furrowed, eyes smouldering like coals. The white man was draped in a cape of unremarkable fabric which fell to his feet. His face was gentle, his eyes soft. He looked like an image of Christ from a calendar. He was immediately recognized.

'Tiradentes! It's Tiradentes,' several voices cried. 'Joaquim José da Silva Xavier, welcome!'

'Viva Tiradentes!' others shouted.

Though they were barefoot, the two men walked towards the pulpit with firm, determined steps. The Black man threw a haughty gaze from one side of the nave to the other. Tiradentes seemed to be staring into space. Rodriguez and I looked in astonishment at this double apparition.

'Tiradentes wasn't disappeared,' I whispered to Rodriguez, 'he was tried and executed in public.'

'But he wasn't given a proper burial,' Rodriguez replied. 'The Portuguese Crown sentenced traitors to be hanged, then quartered, with their heads displayed in a public square. That's what they did to Tiradentes. What's more, his head went missing and was never found, so his spirit feels the same disquiet as we do.'

'And the other guy,' I asked? 'Who's that?'

'Don't you recognize him? That's Zumbi dos Palmares! His majesty Zumbi dos Palmares in fact. They say he was grandson of Princess Aqualtune, the warrior queen of Palmares.'

'Was Zumbi disappeared as well?'

'Not disappeared, but unburied, like Tiradentes. They cut off his head, preserved it with salt and put it on a stake to terrorize the Black population and dispel the belief that he was immortal. And now he's here among us in spirit, immortal, the guardian of his people and a symbol of Black resistance.'

'Have you studied their culture?' I asked.

'A little,' said Rodriguez. 'I know there was a prophecy that a calamity would befall them, causing great suffering. When that happened, a warrior with the strength and courage to liberate them would appear. That warrior was Zumbi.'

Once again I felt ignorant as I listened to Rodriguez's explanation.

'And the trident,' I asked, 'what's the significance of that?'

'It's the trident of Eshu. The three prongs symbolize three vital impulses: sexuality, self-preservation, and spirituality. Eshu is one of the deities in Yoruba mythology. He travels the villages listening to the grievances both of the people and of the orishas. He also brings messages to humans from the other orishas. Zumbi must be here with a message.'

I remembered that Rodriguez had said the spirits of the Indigenous who had been disappeared wouldn't come to the congress, as they inhabited their own cosmogony.

'If the Afro-Brazilians have their own cosmogony, how come Zumbi knew about the congress?'

'It's thanks to their syncretism,' said Rodriguez. 'By associating their orishas with Catholic saints, the Black slaves entered into our Judaeo-Christian cosmogony, but without abandoning their own.'

By this point everyone had realized that the man with Tiradentes was Zumbi dos Palmares. There was a commotion – it was as if an electric current had swept the nave. David invited them to speak, and Tiradentes stepped up to the pulpit. He spoke with a voice which sounded as if it came from the depths of an abyss.

'We are here to claim our place. We were hacked into pieces and our remains were left to the beasts, like some of those gathered here tonight. Just like you, we were given no burial and have no resting place. We too hold sacred the same ideals of freedom. Just like you, I fought for the ideals of the republican revolution: liberty, equality, and fraternity. But my executioners sullied my reputation, they said we rebelled for material reasons, out of greed. It is true that the Portuguese Crown demanded more gold from us than we could provide. But not enough is said about my Enlightenment republican ideals.

'My struggle was for independence and for a secular republic, based on the principles of impartiality, justice, and solidarity – the same values that the fascist mob today wants to erase. There are even monarchists among them, nostalgic for the days of slavery. They have already tried to abolish the national holiday commemorating our uprising; if they had their way, they would strike my name from the history books and from our public squares. They tried to overthrow the republican state once, and they will try again. We came to this meeting to summon you to the fight! The proposals I heard approved here are well intentioned, but words are not enough. It's in the streets and squares where history is made, so I propose a march on Brasília.'

Tiradentes descended from the pulpit to cheers of approval. Then Zumbi ascended the pulpit, speaking in a refined Portuguese incongruous with his appearance, shaking his trident when he became more animated. Rodriguez explained that Zumbi learnt Portuguese from a priest who had abducted him when he was still just a child; it was only later, in Palmares, that he was initiated in the culture and rites of the orishas by a wise man called Djeli.

Zumbi spoke: 'For those who don't know me, I am Zumbi dos Palmares, son of Ogun. My few memories of childhood are confused. I know that I was made captain of arms by my uncle Ganga Zumba, who was poisoned most treacherously. Like him, I am a fighter, a warrior. For fifteen years I fought the bounty hunters. The Palmares quilombo faced eighteen military campaigns, surviving for 110 years. But I'm not here to give you my personal history. I'm here as a messenger of the orishas, to speak on behalf of the thousands of Black people who resisted in Palmares and in so many other quilombos throughout Brazil, of whom so little is said in our schools and our history books. On behalf of those who were tossed into the waters of the Atlantic during the Middle Passage, and those who were flogged and tortured on the whipping post. On behalf of the Black women who were raped by the sugar barons, and the Black soldiers killed in Paraguay, fighting a war which had nothing to do with us, in exchange for promises of emancipation which were never kept. I am here to tell you that all the Black people who have drifted, unburied, will join us here! Slavery was never abolished; it has only changed its shape.'

We had barely had time to absorb these two speeches when a shape appeared in the main entrance to the cathedral and walked resolutely towards us. Another spectre, I thought. Who could this be? As they drew closer to the pulpit I saw they were wearing just a loincloth, but with an elaborate headdress.

'He's Indigenous!' I heard some exclaim.

'A chieftain, a *morubixaba*,' said others. His skin was tanned, his frame muscular, almost like that of a giant. His eyes glowed red like embers. On his forehead he had a crescent-shaped scar. In his right hand was a long spear, with a deadly point. He stood between Zumbi and Tiradentes and raised his left hand, appealing for quiet. After a few moments, he began to speak, slowly, in a southern accent.

'Friends, I have come far, from Sete Povos das Missões, which is why I have arrived so late. I was baptized and confirmed. My Christian name is Joseph and my *nom de guerre* is Sepé Tiaraju, which means Ray of Light. I was saved by the Guarani people after my own people were massacred by the colonizers. Though I was raised to be a shaman, my warrior spirit was too strong, so I became *morubixaba* and chieftain of the warriors of Sete Povos das Missões. Like Zumbi and Tiradentes, I fought for freedom. The colonizers tried to drive us out, but as I told the general, the land on which you walk was given by the gods to our ancestors, who were free, and our children must inherit it free. I faced down 3,700 Spanish and Portuguese soldiers. My hands and my headdress are stained with blood, because I never once bowed to oppression.

'Now, just as they are doing with Tiradentes, they want to appropriate my struggle and my memory. They say I went to heaven, because my body was never found and they want to beatify me. It's a lie. My body was never found because they cut off my head and cremated what remained. I was killed in cowardly fashion, by a shot from an arquebus on the night of a full moon, 7th February 1756. Three days later, they murdered 1,500 of us. These massacres have continued ever since, but I'm here with you because the spirit of liberty is eternal. I'm no saint, no miracle-worker. I belong to no church, nor to the colonizers. I belong to the Guarani people.'

With that, Tiradentes, Zumbi, and Sepé took each other's hands and raised them in a gesture of triumph.

'Didn't you say that the Indigenous wouldn't come?' I asked Rodriguez.

'Indigenous people who have been evangelized inhabit our cosmogony. You heard Sepé say he was baptized and confirmed. In their case, there was no need for syncretism, as the Catholic mythology with all its liturgies and saints overlaps with Indigenous mythology.'

'Had you heard his story?' I asked.

'Yes, in Rio Grande do Sul it's very well known, and Sepé is revered as a hero. There's even an epic poem by Basílio da Gama which glorifies Sepé's fight against the invading forces.'

'I hadn't a clue about any of that.'

'Well, you should know that the Jesuit missions inspired European socialists. It's a remarkable case of a utopian model travelling from one place to another. They were communist societies and were so successful that they were incorporated into the European imaginary, influencing Hegel, the Enlightenment thinkers, utopian socialists, and even anarchists. So much so, that the followers of Babeuf and Blanqui were called red Jesuits by the Parisian workers.'

'Were they really communist?'

'Yes, and prosperous with it. Ownership of the means of production was social, with the incorporation of cooperative practices in hunting already present amongst the Guarani. They had thousands of heads of cattle and cultivated yerba mate, which they exported. They had schools, choirs, and workshops for art, carpentry, even metalwork and printing. The Jesuits made intensive use of art as a means of gradually replacing Indigenous culture with Catholicism.'

'And what happened to them in the end?'

'The colonizer Raposo Tavares took sixteen missions on this side of the River Uruguay and laid them waste. The Jesuits fled, but they later returned and founded Sete Povos das Missões, which became home to around 50,000 Indigenous people. It lasted until 1750, when Spain and Portugal signed a border agreement which placed Sete Povos das Missões in Spanish territory. The Indigenous resisted expulsion from their lands and were attacked by both the Spanish and the Portuguese armies. The ensuing battle was so one-sided that 1,500 Indigenous were killed and just three soldiers. It was a massacre, a genocide.'

15.

And so began the march of the spectres, small at first, little more than 200, but growing in numbers as it moved towards Brasília. We walked slowly, to allow time for other restless spirits to join us. It was a journey of forty days along the tracks and trails of rural São Paulo, Minas Gerais, and Goiás. In the first few days, the spectres of 300 lads disappeared by the Military Police of São Paulo joined the march, almost all of them Black, and some of them little more than boys. Then three boys appeared all holding hands, who had been disappeared in Belford Roxo. One of them was just eight years old. After crossing into Minas another forty young lads who had been disappeared by the local police joined the march, again, most of them Black. There were also three people from Brumadinho who had been disappeared, a man and two women. Then on the outskirts of Brasília, people who had been disappeared by gunmen in Mato Grosso joined our ranks.

Arriving at the Esplanada dos Ministérios, we met the disappeared of the North and Northeast. Peasants murdered in Pará and Maranhão by gunmen in the pay of land-grabbers and wildcat miners. Thousands of subsistence farmers massacred in Canudos, Indigenous people, leaders of the peasant leagues, rural settlers, the disappeared from the Cabanagem and the Contestado War, and three fighters from Araguaia who hadn't turned up to the Congress, Queixada, Nunes, and Cristina. Amarildo the bricklayer was there too.

The Praça dos Três Poderes was teeming with spectres. Groups formed around speakers. At the centre of one was a wiry Black man, hollow-cheeked and with a wispy beard. He wore a military uniform, though it was torn, and he wore no insignia. We listened closely.

'We were cursed even down to our third generation. My brethren were banished, we were decapitated and our heads put on stakes in the square to frighten the people of Bahia. But we will never give in, a time is coming when we will all be brothers. There will no longer be slaves nor kings, and each person will be given their due. Brazil will no longer be a colony, and the soldiers will protect the people instead of just serving the powerful. Viva the people of Brazil! Viva Bahia!'

Emotional, Rodriguez said, 'That must be the soldier Luiz Gonzaga das Virgens, one of the leaders of the Bahian Conspiracy, that was ten years after Tiradentes. Just like him, they rebelled against colonial oppression, but they went further than that – they called not only for a republic, but for the emancipation of the slaves.'

We walked amongst the groups. We noticed a circle of people who were listening rapt to a speech by a frail-looking old man, a Black man with white hair, leaning on a stick. We moved closer. The old man spoke quietly, haltingly, telling his story:

'I was born in the darkest depths of the night and I never submitted to slavery, I fled from the flour and sugar mills of Espírito Santo to the backwoods of Maranhão, I freed more than 1,000, travelling half a league on the way out, another half on the way back; I went on one leg, came back on another. They raised an army to hunt me down. Eight times I was caught and sentenced to hard labour, and eight times I escaped. Three times they killed me and three times I was reborn. I fear nothing, because São Benedito protects me.'

'And do you know who he is?' I asked Rodriguez.

He didn't. 'There were a lot of slave rebellions,' he said, 'but very few of them made it into the history books.'

I asked one of the men in the crowd.

'That's Benedito Meia-Légua,' he said, 'his band was at large in Bahia and Espírito Santo, they made life hell for the mill owners for more than fifty years. It was said that he was invincible.'

'And how was he killed?' I asked.

'They only caught up with him when he was old, sick, and walking with a limp,' said the man. 'He was living in a hollowed-out tree when a hunter denounced him. A slave catcher came, blocked up the tree with mud and then set it on fire. That's what he said, and I believe him.'

Rodriguez wanted to listen to Benedito Meia-Légua's story, so I left him there and strolled up the esplanade. Groups of Indigenous people turned out in headdresses and straw loincloths danced to the sound of bells. I stopped next to a large, close-knit group of peasants, men and women, who had gathered around someone preaching. Gangs of barefoot children surrounded some of the women. The preacher was a peasant too, tall and extremely skinny, scrawny even, wearing a black robe which fell to his shins. He was also barefoot. As he spoke, he gesticulated with one hand, the other resting on a pilgrim's staff. His face was wizened; his beard and hair matted, tangled, falling to his shoulders. When I moved closer, I recognized him: it was the holy man Antônio Conselheiro. I decided to stay and listen to part of his speech. It was a terrible prophecy.

'I was dead, but now I am alive forever more. I looked up and saw a yellow horse, and the rider was called Death, and the world of the dead followed him. The dead were given power over a quarter of the Earth to punish and kill the infidels with hunger, disease, and drought. A terrible catastrophe is coming. Earth will be polluted. The land will become the sea, and the sea will become the land. The sun will become as black as mourning dress, and the moon will become red like blood. One-third of humanity will be killed by five plagues, which will emerge from the depths of the earth: poison, fire, smoke, sulphur, and vermin. They will be wiped off the face of the Earth, not a trace will remain.'

I went back to Rodriguez. He was contemplating the enraptured crowds, a smile on his face. I was reminded of a poem by Manuel Bandeira, and recited a verse under my breath:

> '*A smile glimmered on his tired lip*
> *The subtle, eternal smile of irony*
> *Which will triumph over life and death.*'

'Look how the dead never go quiet,' Rodriguez said. 'Not even those who died ages ago, like Sepé, and all the others that the powerful wanted not only to eliminate physically, but to erase from the popular imaginary, as if they had never existed. They were decapitated, exiled, damned, but now they have rebelled against that same power, with the extraordinary strength of spectres.'

I thought about our meeting a few months beforehand at the Praça da República, where everything had begun. Not by chance, but orchestrated by the Fates, as Rodriguez had concluded.

I asked him, 'Do you think that the true design of the Fates was the Apocalypse of the Spectres, and that our congress was just an instrument?'

'Perhaps,' he said, 'the gods amuse themselves by playing with the destiny of mortals.'

What happened next is another story.

Afterword
Disappear, transitive verb

Though political disappearance has always existed, the concept of *the disappeared* only came to define something in the social imaginary once this sinister method of exterminating political dissidents was adopted in South America between the 1960s and 1970s. By means of complex, clandestine apparatus, criminal states obtained a triple invisibility: of their crimes, of the victims, and of the scale of the policy of extermination.

But the expression has been colonizing other lands. Today, it is everywhere: the waters of the Mediterranean, the grave of thousands of anonymous refugees; the sands of the Sahara, the desert of Arizona, the steppes of Siberia, the mountains of Afghanistan, the cliffs of the Balkans. Who knows where else? There are hundreds, thousands, perhaps millions of disappeared. So many, that the expression has become natural. It is the condition of a body lacking an identity and an identity lacking a body.

Disappearance has a unique impact, both on individual and collective subjectivity. Within families, it generates distress and uncertainty, given the ambiguous situation of simultaneous presence and absence. It is an absence which makes itself present, casting a shadow over mothers and fathers and children and siblings which will last for the rest of their lives, almost like a curse. The meaning of death is also distinct. With disappearance, there is no rupture, no before and afterwards, but a hiatus, a long interval of time containing something unknown, an enigma, a question mark between existence and non-existence, created to conceal a terrible crime.

Within society, a series of disappearances is mysterious, leaving no witnesses, no trace. It thus generates stupor, a feeling that some malign force is at work, which goes beyond the field of reason and the limits of language; a ghostly power, both supernatural and subhuman, seeming to emerge from the very depths of evil. And as the victims belong to a specific group which those in power wish to purge from society, disappearance becomes an instrument of terror. A collective fear is instilled.

The best definition of this newly created phenomenon is attributed to Jorge Rafael Videla, the main architect of the disappearances in Argentina. He coined it spontaneously, in a TV interview upon his return from a visit to Pope John Paul II in 1979. Videla and his generals had estimated that it would be necessary to eliminate from 7,000 to 8,000 Argentine militants in order to preserve the dominant order.

The journalist, José Ignacio López: 'I want to ask if you responded to the Pope and if the government is considering any measures in relation to this issue.'

General Jorge Rafael Videla: 'A disappeared person is per se an unknown quantity. If they appeared, they would receive treatment x, or if this appearance provided certainty of their death then they would receive treatment z, but while they are disappeared they can't receive any special treatment. They are disappeared, a non-entity, neither dead nor alive. In such a situation there's nothing we can do but assist the family.'

We think, we reason, we conceptualize and even dream by means of words. Little by little, society examines its collective traumas. We have words to refer to prisoners, victims of torture, people run over by vehicles, detainees executed in simulated escapes, even people who die by their own hand. But there was no word for those who simply disappear. Objects disappear, clouds disappear, but people don't disappear. They can run away, they can hide, they may be killed, but they don't just disappear involuntarily. The disappeared didn't just vanish; they were kidnapped and then disappeared.

So society created the expression *political disappearance*, though that could – maybe should – have been *political kidnapping* instead. Words don't emerge at random. They express power relations and cognitive phases of the apprehension of reality. At first, the prevalent reaction was simply one of horror at the sudden disappearance of people, but not so much at its mechanisms, which include kidnapping, sensory deprivation, and torture.

And it remained thus. The expression *political disappearance* became, in South and Central America, the symbolic expression of absolute evil, like the apocalypse in biblical narrative, or Auschwitz in modern Europe. It wasn't until later that it produced a field of knowledge and the victim of political disappearance would acquire a legal and political status.

Until that point, none of the dozens of definitions of the verb *to disappear* listed in dictionaries of the Portuguese language had captured this state of affairs, or the spirit of Videla's cynical definition. The grammar books did not classify *to disappear* as a transitive verb and the dictionaries did not list the past participle *disappeared* as a noun. It was thirty years before the Houaiss Dictionary of the Portuguese Language added the following meaning to the past form of the verb *to disappear*: 'Disappeared – noun – a term applied to an individual whose whereabouts are unknown or whose death is presumed, though their body has not been found.'

It is still only an approximation. The entry fails to capture the specific phenomenon of political activists being forcibly disappeared for being political activists. And that at the time of their disappearance, the victims were in the custody of the state, as in the *forced disappearance* (*desaparición forzada*) in the official language of Mexico, and Spain in the post-Franco era, or the more accurate *disappeared detainee* (*detenido desaparecido*), in the official language of Argentina. It still fails to allude to the implicit cruelty and depravity, nor does it capture the condition of the female victims of political disappearance, who suffered a double persecution – both for opposing an oppressive state, and for rejecting the subservient position assigned to women by patriarchal society. In Argentina, they were raped systematically.

The verb *to disappear* is intransitive in its full sense. Like *to die*, it requires no object. But in Portuguese, we use the past participle of the verb *to die* (*morrer*) to say someone *was killed* (*foi morto*), whereas conventionally we don't say he *was disappeared*. We may use phrases like *disappeared from the city*, though how this happened is not given. So we need to go beyond the limits of grammar. Confucius said we should call things by their proper name, so instead of saying someone *was killed*, we should say that he *was murdered*, and instead of saying the tyrant *died by assassination*, we should say he *was executed*.

In this story, the disappeared were not simply killed. They were kidnapped, tortured, deprived of all communication with the outside world, murdered, and only then disappeared. That's why we need to make the verb *to disappear* transitive – as in the examples 'the police *disappeared* someone' or in the passive form 'someone *was disappeared*'. This phrase allows for that function, it implies the existence of a hidden agent, and the recourse to violence. This is unsettling on an individual level, while also alluding to the disturbing effect on the collective unconscious which is generated by sudden and inexplicable disappearances.

The semantics of political disappearance are dynamic, like a disease, a linguistic pathology produced by a social pathology. It acquires new connotations as collective perception evolves. Now and then it returns, with new meaning, generating new fields of knowledge. In law, the concept of transitional justice has emerged, which consists of the demands for truth, justice, and memory for the crime of disappearance, leading to demands for reparatory justice. A new fundamental human right has arisen, the right to truth. A new space for political conflicts has opened up, and new amnesty laws have been passed – like the infamous Full Stop and Due Obedience laws in Argentina.

New biological tools have been developed, like the technique of identifying grandchildren by the DNA of their grandparents, in the absence of their disappeared parents. And these grandchildren constitute a special category of the disappeared, disappeared babies, born in detention and presumably still alive, whose identities, rather than their lives, were stolen.

In criminal justice a new science has emerged, forensic anthropology, with new tools and methods to expose crimes resulting not from the cunning of a criminal individual, but from the limitless power of a terrorist state. And the disappeared reappear as spectres, to haunt the living.

Meanwhile, just like the amnesty decreed at the end of the military dictatorship, the Brazilian courts have absolved the perpetrators of disappearance without even putting them on trial. Unlike in Mexico for example, in Brazilian legal terminology *disappearance* has not been defined as a specific crime. In international conventions it is defined as a crime against humanity, as it impacts the very essence of the human condition, but it does not appear in Brazilian law. It isn't even mentioned in the Law of Public Records (Law 6051), which, while updated several times since it came into force in 1973, still only allows a judge to certify the deaths of those disappeared 'in shipwrecks, floods, fires, earthquakes, and other disasters'.

This oversight also exists in the Civil Code (Law 10,406) of 2002, which allows a judge to declare someone *in absentia* or presumed dead in the following circumstances: '1 – if their life was in danger and their death was very probable; 2 – if they disappear in battle or are taken prisoner, and are still missing two years after the end of the war.' We should add a third condition: 'if they were detained by agents of the state due to their political activity and are still missing two years later.' It is as if the Brazilian lawmaker were also part of this complex machinery which makes people disappear. This is, in fact, the final mechanism: to make someone disappear in law.

Acknowledgements

I would like to thank friends who read versions of this work and provided their feedback: Carlos Tibúrcio, Carlos Knapp, Cláudio Cerri, Ênio Squeff, Flamarion Maués, Gislene Silva, José Genoino, Haroldo Ceravolo Sereza, Joana Monteleone, Paulo Campanário, Sue Branford, and my wife Mutsuko. Special thanks to Zilda Junqueira and Pedro Estevam Pomar for reading and making notes on one of the later versions. I also recognize my debt to Taís Morais and Eumano Silva, authors of *Operação Araguaia*, as well as the valuable work on political disappearance by activists and academics from Argentina, Chile, Peru, Mexico, and Uruguay.

That said, the responsibility for this text is mine alone.

Glossary of Names, Places, and Events

This is not a complete list but aims to assist the reader with brief descriptions of some of the less familiar terms that are not specifically explained in the text.

Álvares Cabral, Pedro	15th century Portuguese nobleman and explorer regarded as the European 'discoverer' of Brazil.
Amarildo	Also known as 'o pedreiro Amarildo' (Amarildo the bricklayer), Amarildo Dias de Souza was kidnapped and disappeared by police in the Rocinha favela in Rio de Janeiro in 2013. As of 2025, his remains have never been found.
Amazonas, João	Also known as 'Cid', or 'Velho Cid', a member of the Brazilian Communist Party (PCB) from the 1930s, later founder and leader of the Communist Party of Brazil (PCdoB), and liaison between the party leadership and the guerrilla force in Araguaia.

Amnesty Law	Passed by Congress in August 1979, the Lei da Anistia was an important milestone on Brazil's return to democracy, leading to the release of political prisoners and the return of nearly 2,000 exiles. However, it also conferred immunity from prosecution on all military and police personnel guilty of human rights abuses during the country's 1964–85 military dictatorship.
Araguaia campaign	Between 1966 and 1974, members of the PCdoB (at the time of Maoist orientation) tried to establish a rural stronghold to wage a guerrilla war against the military dictatorship.
Arraes, Miguel	Mayor of Recife, then governor of Pernambuco state. Imprisoned, then exiled by the military government, he returned to Brazil in 1979.
Assault on the Three Branches of Government	Brazil's Congress, Supreme Court, and Presidential Palace were attacked on 8th January 2023 by a mob of supporters of Jair Bolsonaro, following their leader's defeat in the presidential elections in October 2022.
Babeuf, François Noël	1760–97, also known as Gracchus Babeuf, was a French revolutionary and 'proto-communist'.
Blanqui, Louis Auguste	1805–81 was a French socialist and political philosopher.
Cabanagem	A revolutionary and separatist movement in Grão-Pará province, 1835–40. It was eventually crushed by the Brazilian military. It is estimated that 30–40% of the 100,000 inhabitants of the province were killed in the conflict.
Cachaça	A strong, distilled cane spirit or *aguardente* popular in Brazil.

Campos dos Goytacazes	The Cambahyba sugar mill at Campos dos Goytacazes in Rio de Janeiro state was used to cremate the bodies of disappeared prisoners between 1973 and 1975, among them probably David Capistrano.
Canudos	A settlement in the interior of the north-eastern state of Bahia, founded in 1893 as the centre of a millenarian grassroots Catholic movement. Identifying Canudos as a threat to the Republic's ideas of order and progress, the Brazilian state waged four military campaigns against it. In the last of these, in October 1897, the army slaughtered 25,000 of its residents and destroyed the community.
Capistrano, David	Leader of the Brazilian Communist Party (PCB), who fought in the International Brigades in Spain, and later in the French Resistance. He was arrested, tortured, and disappeared in March 1974 in Rio de Janeiro. He was probably executed in the Casa da Morte in Petrópolis and his body either thrown into a river or incinerated at the Cambahyba sugar mill.
Cid	*see* Amazonas, João
Conselheiro, Antônio	Leader of a millenarian cult in the northeastern state of Bahia, which founded the settlement of Canudos.
Contestado War	A guerrilla war (1912–16) for land between landowners and settlers, in the southern states of Paraná and Santa Catarina. The monk and healer José Maria de Santo Agostinho led an uprising against the republican government, which eventually ended in a massacre of the insurgents.

Da Gama, Basílio	A colonial Brazilian poet, author of the famous epic poem *O Uraguai* (1769). This depicts the Portuguese and Spanish military campaign of 1756 against the Sete Povos indigenous mission settlements administered by the Jesuits in southern Brazil, ending in the deaths of over 1,500 Guarani people.
Due Obedience Law	The Ley de Obediencia Debida was passed in Argentina in June 1987. A complement to the Full Stop Law, it exempted all ranks of the armed forces and security services from punishment for crimes committed during the dictatorship. It was repealed in 2003.
Economic Miracle	The 'Milagre Econômico Brasileiro' was a period of exceptional economic growth during the dictatorship, especially from 1969 to 1973. However, this ultimately proved unsustainable, and by the end of the military regime, Brazil was struggling with high inflation, unemployment, and one of the world's largest external debts.
Esplanada dos Ministérios	Part of the Monumental Axis, the main avenue in the centre of Brasília, with the Praça dos Três Poderes at one end.
Estado Novo	The Third Republic period in Brazil (1937–46) under the authoritarian presidency of Getúlio Vargas.
Fazendeiro, Pedro	Pedro Inácio de Araújo, known as Pedro Fazendeiro, was a shoe-maker, peasant leader, and friend of Nego Fubá.
Foco theory	Popularized by Che Guevara and elaborated by Regis Debray, it held that a small group of guerrilla activists, based in the countryside, could ignite a revolutionary overthrow of the existing regime.

Franco, Marielle   A Brazilian politician, sociologist, feminist, socialist, and human rights activist, shot dead in her car along with her driver in Rio on 14th March 2018. In 2024 two former police offers were convicted of her murder and given lengthy prison sentences.

Fuba, Nego   João Alfredo Dias, known as Nego Fubá, was a Black peasant leader involved in the struggle for land reform in Paraíba State.

Full Stop Law   The Ley de Punto Final, passed by the Argentine Congress in 1986 to end the investigation and prosecution of security and military officers for crimes committed during the dictatorship. It was repealed in 2003 and declared unconstitutional in 2005.

Herzog, Vladimir   A prominent journalist and member of the Communist Party, Herzog was arrested in October 1975 and tortured. The military claimed he had hanged himself in his cell, but few believed them. It became a cause celèbre, contributing to the eventual end of the dictatorship.

Jesuit Missions   Settlements established by the Jesuit Order straddling the borders with Argentina, Paraguay, and Brazil. They had their origins in the 16th century and ended in the late 18th century when the Jesuits were expelled from the Americas. They were generally more progressive than other parts of the colonial system and attempted to give some autonomy to Indigenous peoples, especially the Guarani.

Joaquim	Codename of Ângelo Arroyo, member of the PCdoB Central Committee and second-in-command of the Araguaia campaign. He managed to escape the army repression, one of only a handful of survivors. He was killed in the Lapa Massacre in 1976.
Jonas, Comandante	Virgílio Gomes da Silva (Comandante Jonas) was a member of the ALN and one of the group which kidnapped the American Ambassador Charles Burke Elbrick on 4th September 1969. Jonas was captured shortly afterwards, tortured, killed, and disappeared.
José Maria	(monk) *see* Contestado War
Lamarca, Carlos	Carlos Lamarca was a Brazilian army captain who deserted to join the armed struggle against the dictatorship. He was killed by the army in 1971.
Lampião	Virgulino Ferreira da Silva, ('Lampião') led a band of up to 100 *cangaceiros* (bandits) in Northeast Brazil in the 1920s and 1930s.
Lapa Massacre	In December 1976, the Brazilian police machine-gunned a house on Rua Pio XI, São Paulo, killing three leaders of the PCdoB and taking several others prisoner.
Malê rebellion	A religious and racial uprising in Bahia which began in 1835. Led by African Muslims, it was one of the most important uprisings against slavery in Brazilian history.
Mangueira	A Rio de Janeiro neighbourhood, home to one of the most famous samba schools which competes in carnival.

Marchinha	A Brazilian genre of music for carnival that satirizes military marches and other pomp.
Marighella, Carlos	Founder of Ação Libertadora Nacional, an urban guerrilla group, in 1967. He had been active in leftist politics for more than thirty-five years. He was ambushed and shot dead by police in São Paulo on 4th November 1969.
Middle Passage	The second leg of the triangular trade in which manufactured goods were shipped from Europe to Africa; then slaves were shipped to the Americas; finally plantation products such as sugar, rum, and tobacco were shipped to Europe.
National Liberation Action	Led by Carlos Marighella, Ação Libertadora Nacional (ALN) was a guerrilla group formed in 1967 by dissidents from the PCB.
National Truth Commission	The Comissão Nacional de Verdade (CNV) was set up in 2012 to investigate serious human rights violations in Brazil in the period 1945–88. It lasted two years, until December 2014.
Orishas	(also orixás) Divine spirits in the Yoruba religion of West Africa and in diaspora religions that derive from it, including Candomblé in Brazil.
Pais-de-santo	Also known as Babalorixás or Babas, the priests of Candomblé, a religion that developed in Brazil combining elements of several African religions and cultures with some Catholic beliefs and practices. Mainly urban, its centre is in Salvador, Bahia, but it is found in all major cities.

Paiva, Rubens	A civil engineer, elected to Congress for São Paulo in 1962, he went into exile in 1964. After returning to Rio de Janeiro, he was detained at his house by the military in 1971 with his wife and daughter. He was tortured and killed at an air force base. His body was never found.
Paraguayan War	An exceptionally bloody territorial conflict, also known as the War of the Triple Alliance, 1864–70, fought between Paraguay and the Triple Alliance of Argentina, the Empire of Brazil, and Uruguay.
Pau de arara	The 'parrot's perch', a brutal torture method favoured by the dictatorship. The victim is tied by the ankles and wrists and strung up, usually naked, on a horizontal pole, forcing them into a stress position from which there is no possible relief. It causes severe pain and psychological trauma.
Peasant Leagues	Founded in the 1940s and 1950s by communists, socialists, and others, the ligas camponesas were social movements formed to advocate for the interests of small-scale farmers, particularly in Northeast Brazil.
Pinto, Onofre	A mechanic, former soldier, and guerrilla fighter, member of the Vanguarda Popular Revolucionária group, disappeared in 1974.
Pomar, Pedro	Founder and leader of the PCdoB, killed by the police in 1976 in the Lapa Massacre.
Popular Liberation Movement	Movimento de Libertação Popular (Molipo) was a dissident section of National Liberation Action (ALN). Most of its members had been killed by 1974.

Popular Revolutionary Vanguard	Vanguarda Popular Revolucionária (VPR), a Marxist-Leninist guerilla organization, formed in 1966 to oppose the military dictatorship and eventually establish a socialist republic. By 1973 it had largely been dismantled.
Protracted people's war	A revolutionary Maoist strategy developed by Mao Zedong and adopted in 1966 by the PCdoB. It signified a long-term, rural-based armed struggle that gradually encircles and overthrows urban centres to achieve political power.
Quilombo	Communities of escaped slaves and others in colonial Brazil. The most well-known is Palmares, which developed from 1605 until its suppression in 1694. It was located in the captaincy of Pernambuco, in what is now Alagoas state.
Samba-enredo	An extended theme song, chosen by each samba school to accompany its parade in the carnival competition.
Sete Povos das Missões	Seven indigenous settlements established by Spanish and Portuguese Jesuits in the frontier region of Rio Grande do Sul from 1682 onwards.
Tiradentes	Joaquim José da Silva Xavier, known as 'Tiradentes', was a leader of the revolutionary movement called the Inconfidência Mineira (1789–92), which aimed to win independence from Portugal and found a republic. The plot was betrayed and Tiradentes was imprisoned in Rio and hanged in 1892. Now regarded as a founding hero of Brazil, the anniversary of his death is a national holiday.

Tuti	Nickname of Stuart Angel Jones, a member of the MR8 guerrilla group, who was arrested, tortured, and killed on 14th July 1971, and his body subsequently disappeared.
Years of Lead	The Anos de Chumbo were the most repressive period of the military dictatorship, following the passing of Institutional Act No. 5 (AI–5) in December 1968, which suspended most civil rights in Brazil. This period lasted until 1974.
Zumba, Ganga	First leader of the 17th century community of escaped slaves, the Palmares Quilombo.
Zumbi dos Palmares	Last leader of the 17th century community of escaped slaves, the Palmares Quilombo.

9 781788 534222